The Teachers Will Save U.S.

José Rodelgo-Bueno

The
Teachers
Will Save U.S.

HAB

Human Adventure Books, Denver

José Rodelgo-Bueno
The Teachers Will Save U.S.

ISBN:978-0-9823561-6-6

to all teachers

Contents

Introduction

Undervalued, vilified, unsupported, stressed, underpaid, yet still undeterred. Unsung heroes, generously giving of themselves, against all odds, fighting a silent, difficult battle with immense sacrifice, tenacity, and perseverance. This battle - the battle of educating the men and women of tomorrow - takes place daily in our schools. Now more than ever, teaching has become a true calling or vocation - a call to remedy the bleak future that many foresee. The economic crisis and the tumultuous international climate have propelled teachers into the forefront, making them indispensable in the struggle to save our children and our nation. In their hands rests the American dream, economic progress, social stability, and world peace.

We cannot rely on the government and politicians to fix everything that is wrong. Government policies and reforms can provide some relief, but there are fundamental issues that government and politics cannot solve; it is society's responsibility to act. The change needed now must begin from the bottom up, with the people - individuals, families, teachers, schools, and social groups. This change will not materialize out of thin air. It is a mentality that is cultivated and transmitted through education, from person to person, from generation to generation. Without true education, there cannot be a sustainable quality of life.

Educators are the key to initiating this transformation. It seems like an insurmountable task, but teachers do not shy away or despair in the face of challenges. Through their veins courses the blood of our forefathers, who after arriving on the Mayflower adapted to a hostile environment to cultivate the land and build homes, businesses, schools, and our great nation. They made something great out of nothing. Our nation's forefathers had a great ideal, and this impelled them to face difficult circumstances with hope, viewing them as opportunities for change. They saw challenges as opportunities to enhance their creativity and intellect and were not afraid of making sacrifices. Through these challenges, they increased their solidarity with one another and their desire to create a common good. Our country has forged ahead as a world leader due to the ingenuity, courage, and perseverance of its citizens.

That ideal is not dead. We are part of that great tradition. Teachers are fundamental in perpetuating the ideal and keeping that tradition alive by forming generations of people with passion for knowledge, with insatiable initiative, with creativity, with love for liberty and peace, and with a generosity that embraces the outcasts of society and expresses compassion for the needy. The youth have the right to have hope in the future.

Everyone acknowledges the need for education in such a difficult time in history. The question is, "How?" The issue at hand is finding the appropriate method of education. In this country, many educational reforms have been implemented in the last hundred years, but these reforms have not tackled the root of the problem. Why? Because these reforms have never taken into account the human aspect of education. There cannot be true education if the humanity of the student is not addressed.

What changes and renews our humanity is also what renews society. Society can only be renewed by people who have been renewed, by authentic human beings. A teacher is able to bring out the best in the student by inviting the student to grow with him in the learning process. In fact, when teachers live an experience of teaching that is incessantly generating their inner being, they communicate a fullness of life. When they do so, this humanity overflows from their hearts, through osmosis, making their students' humanity thrive.

Teachers have access to a student's inner self, and therefore can encourage growth and initiate change. There is no one like the teacher who can foster the growth of the student's sense of freedom and responsibility. The teacher can help the student understand himself, discover a sense of dignity and his true potential. The teacher can help the student not to despair during difficult times, but to see life's challenges as an opportunity to grow. At the same time, the teacher is the one who can help the student understand reality, and he does this by considering the student as worthy of discovering the world, counting the student's observations as valid. This type of education does not appear on the "standards lists" or in "standardized testing", but it is, in fact, vital. This type of education is a human experience that must be lived.

Many administrators and teachers in public, charter, private, and religious schools would like to implement an education worthy of the challenges of the 21st century, the education needed to overcome the human crisis we are facing. However, the majority of them do not know how. They lack the right method. This book could help by answering the following questions:

- How do we educate the entire human being?

- How do we teach human beings to understand themselves so that they can better understand the world?

- What kind of education is needed to properly understand a global and complex world?

In this book you will find the method needed, as well as concrete examples, of how to implement a system that works. Although I recognize the benefits of a liberal arts education and a liberal arts curriculum, it is not the purpose of this book to promote them. The goal of this book is to describe a method - the educational method needed to face this human crisis and to help human beings to understand themselves and the world. The only way to do so is by teaching people to grow in self-awareness and the awareness of reality as a whole. If we want to build a more human world, we must first discover what it truly means to be human. There is a mystery within us and behind each aspect of reality, and it is visible every day in the news, in our families, in our schools, and in every single subject of the curriculum. This method is an educational journey to the truth of things and to the truth of life's fundamental issues.

Education does not mean sending our children to school every day. We are in the midst of a human crisis, and therefore education concerns us all. Teachers are not the only educators, and children are not the only ones in need of education. In education, we all participate. Education is the communication of a human experience; it is life's experience within a lived experience. This experience can be lived in our schools, as well as in any other educational relationship, be it teacher-student, parent-child, or peer-to-peer.

Although this book is intended primarily for administrators, teachers, and parents involved in the education of middle and high school students, this book can be useful for college students and professors as well. This method works in all aspects of education, including school life, all the disciplines of the curriculum, and family life. For this reason I provide some criteria and examples for every subject matter to help teachers modify their lesson plans in a way that will allow them to engage their students along a journey to the depths of reality and their own humanity.

The first chapter discusses the crisis at hand. The crisis that we are living is much more than just economic, political, or social. It is a human crisis that concerns what defines and moves human beings. Therefore, educators have a crucial role because it is through education that we can address the crisis.

The second chapter discusses the various definitions of education; a number of synonyms are used to refer to this concept, each with a distinct connotation. Education cannot be reduced to entertaining students or training them to enter a good college or obtain a job. When the curriculum is significantly modified to attend the social demands of the youth or markets, we can end up oversimplifying traditional subject matters and providing supermarket-style schooling. At the same time, we cannot forget the importance of cultivating the human dimension through the curriculum and providing a viewpoint so that students can grow in self-awareness.

The third chapter develops the concept of experience. The study starts with John Dewey's concept of learning, for which education must be based on experience. The study then progresses toward the growth of the child in self-awareness and the awareness of particular realities and reality as a whole. Education is more than teaching students to learn by doing; it is a human experience.

The fourth chapter discusses the method required for education to be lived as a human and integral experience. This method was developed by Luigi Giussani, one of the greatest educators of the 20th century. The book is a practical application of his thought. This chapter references him extensively. Giussani's method can be summarized by saying that the journey to truth is an experience. The educator provides a proposal, which is our culture, and it is embedded in the curriculum. The student must then test the proposal using his reason and his freedom within his environment.

What kind of school does the human being need in this crucial moment in history? Certainly, a different type of school is needed. This is the theme of the fifth chapter. Vision, academics, assessment, guidance, discipline, diversity, and a variety of other aspects of school life are discussed.

The final chapter provides some ideas that school administrators can use to improve curriculum and academic planning, as well as ideas to help teachers enhance their lesson plans and educational activities in order to foster student self-awareness, interdisciplinary connections, and awareness of our intricate world.

Finally, I would like to acknowledge the suggestions that more than fifty teachers, administrators, and researchers gave me. I extend my deepest gratitude to all of them. Now, I would like to continue this dialogue with the readers, and I welcome suggestions and criticisms. My hope is that after reading this book, readers will have a deeper understanding of the importance of a human education. My goal is to encourage readers to live this fascinating experience and to share it, hopefully, with me too.

Chapter 1
The Crisis at Hand

Human Crisis

We are living in a crucial moment in history. Unemployment, public debt, political divisions, and poverty are plaguing this nation, and while economic reforms and political compromises can provide some short-term relief, they will not solve the crisis. The root of the problem is neither economic nor sociological; it is human. It is an anthropological crisis because it concerns what defines human beings, what moves human beings – their longings. In this sense, it is an educational crisis, because it is through education that we can renew what is human in us. However, this country has attempted many educational reforms in the last century without arriving at the heart of the problem. If we want to renew our society, we must rediscover true education. Our goal cannot be solely to achieve better academic results or better pedagogical methods. Our goal must be the education of our humanity.

This crisis offers a great opportunity for change. We must rebuild society by building true human beings, because what renews our humanity is also what renews society. We need people who build families, companies, houses, schools, and society; people who help other people and create jobs; people who are proud of their identity, but who are able to embrace people with other identities; people who see reality in its depth; people who seek the common good for our country and peace in the world. To achieve this goal, we need an education that cannot be found in a book. This type of education is an experience, a human experience.

Let us look at some signs of this human crisis. My goal is not to depict a pessimistic perspective of our society but rather to point to some symptoms that can help us to diagnose it. Once diagnosed, we can address the problem and work together to effect real change.

A glance to our economy points us to some of the symptoms. In the past, entrepreneurs invested their money to build productive companies and create employment. At a certain point, many of them began to prefer speculation to obtain quick and better returns. This had important economic consequences, but it was not an economic issue in itself. Rather, it was a human issue. We cannot fight unemployment if people lose their will to build companies; thus, we must provide reasons for entrepreneurs to create companies and generate jobs. Economic policies and stimulus are not enough; the future of our country relies on our capacity to reawaken the ideals of our people and to support the initiative of those who want to generate industry and society. True human beings engage reality with longings for fulfillment and fruitfulness, with a desire to help others, and with a desire to build a better world.

We went too far in our deregulation of banks and financial institutions. We gave them too much power, favoring a culture of speculation over a culture of production and generation. Consciously or unconsciously, we formed bubbles that did not reflect reality. For some years we did not care much about it, because we thought that the new economy of the '90s could continue growing indefinitely. Now we have realized that the common good is not being pursued and that poverty and economic inequalities are increasing. It seems that globalization is not being managed by the democratically elected political powers, but rather by financial institutions and global markets.

Although there have been scandals in which business executives were taking advantage of their employees and shareholders, the economic crisis is not merely an ethical crisis. Regarding the economy, there is a great misconception about the definition of the focus of the economy versus the goal of the economy. The focus of the economy should be the human being, whereas the goal of the economy and financial institutions should be to serve the common good. Among the people who provoked this economic crisis and those who have unsuccessfully tried to solve it, there have been great and very ethical economists. However, their knowledge about the economy proved to be flawed. Economists flood the daily news with data, but they are unable to provide meaningful insight concerning qualitative issues about human beings, such as their needs and human longings. Economists are bad economists if they are only economists. Their information can be accurate from the mathematical point of view, but it will never be useful if it is not accurate from the human point of view as well. This explains why economists differ in their predictions, why they are unable to foresee economic crises, and why they are unable to lead us out of them; they do not comprehend that the root of the problem is not economic but human.

The human crisis can be seen in the political arena as well, especially in our politicians' inability to work together for the common good. Another issue is that many politicians promise things that they know in advance they will not be able to deliver. They are often more interested in obtaining power than in serving our country. All of this incites within the people a lack of confidence in our public institutions and provokes a big economic and social impact, yet the root of this problem remains primarily human, not political.

Another sign of the human crisis is the growing intergenerational conflict that affects Western societies. In our country, the retirement of large numbers of baby boomers, unemployment, fewer opportunities for the youth, and differing opinions about how to use public funds create growing social unrest. Different generations will compete for the assistance of an under-funded government. The problem will be aggravated if what is happening in Europe begins to take place here. It seems that Europeans do not want to have children, which is another sign of the human crisis. A low birth rate implies that less people have to contribute more to support a larger ageing population.

This intergenerational conflict can also be looked at from other perspectives such as the environment, immigration, distribution of wealth, or international relations. In light of these issues, we cannot say that we will leave a better legacy to the next generations than the one we received. We can try to blame many external or contingent factors, but there is no doubt that the society we are creating is less human, and we have to acknowledge that we share part of the responsibility for that transformation.

Through the global media, the dominant culture presents an anthropology that is far from our stature as human beings. It is popular to love ecology, respect nature, and protect the environment. However, it seems that it is not popular to listen to human nature and respect it. Media and technology spread confusion around truths, and little by little, our legal system is taking steps in that same direction, disregarding the supremacy of natural law over civil law. As there is no way to know what is true and what is human, we are unable to set universal values; thus, every opinion has the same worth. The problem with this, as we have seen throughout history, is that some majorities – such as Nazism and Marxism – can be cruel. For this reason, relativism cannot be accepted. Indeed, Albert Einstein – the discoverer of the theory of relativity – denounced the concept of relative truth saying that the relativistic viewpoint is incorrect when dealing with moral decisions.[1]

The human crisis is visible in our youth. Many people say that our teenagers and our youth are passive; they are noncommittal, they delay making important life decisions, and they prefer "to leave all doors open". Why is this? It is because the lack of certainty, which stems from a belief in relative truth, provokes a lack of hope in them. Thus, they lack energy, passion, and affection.

However, the human crisis in the youth cannot be separated from the human crisis in adults; both are immersed in the same dominant mentality. The evidence of this is the instability of family life. Many children have seen that nothing lasts, not even the most sacred of relations such as that of the family. The human crisis concerns us all, because only if adults are mature can they teach children to be mature. Phillip Blond, a driving force behind the British Prime Minister David Cameron, believed that the root of the crisis is the erosion of human relationships. In his opinion, the economy could never have collapsed the way it did without a prior collapse of human relationships such as the family and the social bonds needed to build the common good of a nation. Blond said, "the two dominant political ideologies in the West, socialism and capitalism, have not differed, in that, with respect to the priority of relationships, they adopted exactly the same form; they both erode family, culture, and social unity."[2]

We no longer understand our longings and desires. Desires are what move our society, our culture, our markets, and our media. Polls, media analysts, and consumer experts think they know what drives us. However, the human being "has become insatiable, so accustomed to having his desires satisfied that he can no longer get enough, cannot even decide what he wants, doesn't know what to do with himself, has lost the run of himself."[3] The most dangerous threat to the world is not a calamity from the outside. Mankind will stop generating, inventing, and producing if it losses the zest for living.[4] Our desires can confuse us, lead us to desperation, and destroy us. However, if they are properly clarified and educated, they become our hope. The question is, then, who can educate our longings? Who can give us hope?

Relativism and all of these symptoms of human passivity and confusion are not primarily a religious or ethical problem, but a crisis of humanity. Our country is suffering from this human crisis, even though religion and values are still present in the daily life of Americans. Nietzsche believed that religion was not finished, but that it regardless did not have the capacity to move people.[5] The United States is a very religious country, and certain groups are increasingly active and visible. However, more and more faith is perceived as irrelevant to life's needs. When faith is reduced to only doctrine or ethics, it loses its capacity to guide us as we face life's challenges. Faith is relegated to the privacy of our conscience and some rituals performed on Sunday. Thus, in the end, a person's faith, or the lack thereof, matters little, because almost everybody makes decisions based on the same criteria – the media and the dominant culture. However, it is in this critical moment of history when a true education must show its capacity to help the new generations understand their lives and the world.

Educational Crisis

We are not living through a primarily educational crisis. The educational crisis that we face is a consequence of the human crisis. The crisis of our human nature has developed a crisis of human life, a crisis of social life. As a consequence of the social life crisis, we find ourselves in the midst of an educational crisis. Human crises become social crises and social crises generate educational crises. However, it is through education that we can overcome the root of the problem, the human crisis. Thus, this is a great opportunity for change.

As we said before, the first step will be to diagnose the problem. Once the problem is diagnosed, we will consider ways to address it. First of all, we have to determine why our society and our educational system are unaware, impassive, incapable, ashamed, or afraid of facing the human crisis that we are living today. Among other reasons for this failure, we can mention the following:

1. There is a widespread anthropological error, a misconception of what the human being is. The person is reduced to a kind of biological mechanism and is defined by the findings of pedagogical, psychological, and social research.

2. A warped conception of success, when combined with our individualistic culture, portrays a distorted perspective of a person's value.

3. We are so focused on concrete aspects of education such as standards, testing, and finance, that we lose perspective of the whole picture; we forget education's true purpose.

4. Very often, education is manipulated and becomes an instrument of political wars or the place of social unrest.

5. There is a loss of authority in the family and in school. Part of that authority went to the media.

6. Education no longer aims to introduce people to the meaning of the world and existence.

Let us develop each of these issues to discover the root problem and propose a way to face the crisis.

Education has been the field in which reformers and researchers have experimented with innumerable pedagogical, psychological, and social techniques. Diane Ravitch, a renowned educational expert of our time and former U.S. assistant secretary of education, believes that during the last century, there have been many unsuccessful attempts to improve education through the introduction of new pedagogical methods, new ways to enhance learning through technologies, new assessments, new ways to improve school administration and organize classrooms, and new motivational initiatives. In her words, "In every instance, reformers believed that their solution was the very one that would transform the schools, make learning fun, raise test scores, and usher in an age of educational joy or educational efficiency."[6] In response to the famous question of why Johnny can't read, Hannah Arendt ironically answered that it is because our country is the most advanced and the most modern in the world: "Nowhere else have the most modern theories in the realm of pedagogy been so uncritically and slavishly accepted."[7]

Why have we repeatedly made the same mistake for more than a hundred years? We can find the answer in the prophetic words of Niebuhr, for whom the error of modern educators consists of the assumption that our social problems come from the incapacity of social sciences to follow the progress of physical sciences: "The invariable implication of this assumption is that with a little more time, a little more adequate moral and social pedagogy and a generally higher development of human intelligence, our social problems will approach solution."[8]

Many people talk about the importance of education for developing human capital. But, what is real human capital?

How do we develop it? For more than a century, thousands of researchers, new technologies, new techniques, and incredible amounts of resources have been devoted to the improvement of our educational system. We cannot deny that there are psychologists, social workers, researchers, technological resources, pedagogical methods and techniques, standards, and procedures present in our classrooms. Why have all of these resources failed? First, it is because the teacher and the student are human beings and thus, they have freedom. The second reason is that the human being cannot be reduced to a mechanism that follows certain pedagogical, psychological, and social laws. Deeply rooted in all of those reforms and research was an anthropological mistake, a misconceived notion of what the person was, and what education was.

Einstein points to the second root of our human and educational crisis: "Everywhere, in economic as well as in political life, the guiding principle is one of ruthless striving for success at the expense of one's fellow men. This competitive spirit prevails even in school."[9] Very often success is not based on the idea of merit or the will to produce and be fruitful; rather it is based on destructive ambition or on the fear that people will not accept us. The consequence is the erosion of human cooperation and the common good. We impose goals on ourselves that many times are almost impossible to reach, and with all our human willpower we desperately strive to bring them into being.[10] Graduations in our schools and colleges spread a mentality in which it seems that the value of the student is the success achieved. "That is where man is to place his hope; he is to bank on his own energy. Whether in this or that field, what matters is to make life a success."[11] This anthropological view of education is wrong. The dignity and the value of a person do not depend on her success. Every person has infinite value. In saying this, I am not claiming that success is something bad. Success is good. What I am saying is that one's happiness cannot depend only on his success. Success does not have the power to completely satisfy one's infinite longing for fulfillment. The ruthless striving for success and accumulation of things or power cannot fulfill us.

What is at stake is our conception of the human being. Without an adequate idea of the human being we cannot understand goodness or what the common good of our society really means. We have to admit that individualism does not work, and it can lead to desperate solitude: a person with no real relationships with people, with things, and with himself.[12] We have to admit that we cannot fulfill ourselves on our own. We always need another. We can only truly love ourselves and truly love others if we have first been loved with an infinite and gratuitous love.

The third reason for our failure to face the human crisis relates to the fact that we have placed such an emphasis on standards, testing, and other concrete aspects that we have forgotten the goal of education. I favor improving the efficiency of the educational system, in particular during these times of economic crisis, when we have to use all of our resources as effectively as possible. I agree with those who believe in the importance of standards and standardized testing, and with those who believe that we should do more to help our students achieve better academic results. We have to realize that since the Soviet launch of the Sputnik in 1957, the quality of our educational system has been criticized. Reagan's "A Nation at Risk" report in 1983 again denounced our system, and the PISA international tests that compare academic achievement in OECD (Organization for Economic Development and Cooperation) countries remind us every year that achievement in our schools needs to improve. However, some people believe that education in this country can be fixed by collecting data and applying business principles to the educational system.[13] Instead of leading to a renewed focus on the true meaning of education, certain concrete aspects of education could become ends in themselves.

The implementation of the Common Core Standards and the College and Career Readiness Standards are a clear example of the failure to face this human crisis. I acknowledge the importance of these standards, which address comprehensive content and application of knowledge through high-order skills. They are transnationally benchmarked to enable all students to be prepared to succeed in our global world. However, the standards do not include the human aspect of education and do not foster the human fulfillment of our students. The aim of these standards should coincide with the true purpose of education.

The fourth reason for our incapacity to deal adequately with the human crisis relates to the use of education as the place for ideological and political confrontations. The root of this problem can be found in the fact that there has always been a large influx of immigrants in our country. According to Feinberg and Soltis, "reformers in the United States looked to the schools as a major instrument for assimilating new groups into what was called the American way of life."[14] The problem is that "when this is done, some people get uncomfortable with the idea of manipulating people to achieve social ends."[15] Since the years of Rousseau, education has been such a powerful instrument in the hands of politicians that many of them cannot resist the temptation to use it to indoctrinate others or to obtain political gains.

In addition, the separation of Church and State – far from the spirit of what our constitutional fathers wanted – provides the State with the opportunity to impose in our public schools a certain worldview and set of ethics. Students are introduced to a particular presentation of the world, social issues, politics, personal relations, affection, or family life. They are introduced to a specific perspective of what the person is, and many times this perspective conflicts with the one that parents want for their children.

Progressive education and constructivism helped the State diminish the authority of parents and teachers. On the one hand, reformers tried to implement a world of children emancipated from adults – similar to the emancipation of workers and women – destroying the elementary conditions of life needed for their growth and development. On the other hand, constructivism, with the goal of helping children to build their own knowledge, reduced the authority of teachers by transforming them into mediators.[16] Teachers not only lost part of their authority, but they lost a great part of their prestige and social recognition, too.

The loss of authority is linked with the crisis in culture and tradition. Many parents and teachers are no longer able to transmit our culture and beliefs to the children. That is why children grow up disoriented, without a criterion with which to understand themselves and the world. Part of the authority lost by parents and teachers went to the media.[17] Obviously those in power and the dominant mentality use the media to impose a certain culture, a certain alienating and dehumanizing worldview. This is the culture in which the last generations grew up, and this is the culture in which our children are growing up today.

The goal of education is no longer to introduce the person to the meaning of reality and human existence. The human being is not a dog that we train or a hard drive that we fill with information. The main goal of education should be to help the person grow as a human being, to help develop and increase his humanity. After an academic year, students can point to all of the theorems and formulas they have learned. We can measure their results, process the data, and congratulate ourselves on the improvement shown through standardized testing. However, what did they learn about the meaning of life and about themselves as individuals? Is there a way to test that? In the educational system, it is impossible to avoid the human aspect and the mystery behind it. Yet for true education to occur, teachers must transmit their humanity, and students must share their humanity as well. A true education is an education of what is human in us.[18] When a child or a young person, moved by the desire to know, exposes his inner self by asking a question, then the adult can help him to discover the path to the fulfillment of that desire. When teenagers share their humanity, they are exposed to the arrows with which beauty, goodness, and truth wound their inner being. Thus, developing the student's awareness of life and existence is the most important aspect of education and cannot be disregarded.

After diagnosing the problem, we have to propose ways to address it. We said that it is through education that we will overcome this human crisis. However, what kind of education is needed? What is true education? What education truly matches our human nature? To answer these questions we have to analyze what education is.

Chapter 2

What Is Education?

The word "education" can mean many different things. The way we use this word communicates a different sense of its overall meaning. We encounter a problem, however, because everyone thinks he already knows what education means. Analyzing the etymology of the word "education" can help us find its true meaning.

Education comes from the Latin "educo" (-ducere – duxi –ductum), which means "to draw out," "to lead out." Education entails drawing out something that is inside the student and leading the student to a destiny. "Educo" also means "to raise up." In this sense, to educate is to help someone grow up, not only physically but also in all dimensions. It entails helping every aspect of the person to mature. The etymology of the word "formation" – which we often use instead of education –, significantly changes the meaning, because it implies the shaping of the person according to an external plan, similar to the introduction of new software in a computer.[19]

With honorable and not-so-honorable intentions, many ideologists throughout history, particularly after the

French Revolution, have used the educational system to shape children's "hard drives" according to their ideas. In *Democracy and Education*, Dewey, the greatest American educational theorist, states that education is the primary method of social efficiency and reform, and that "social efficiency is nothing less than socialization of mind."[20] Cremin, in one of the best brief histories of American education, says, "Whereas Emerson had looked forward to the day when education would supplant politics, Dewey announced that the day had already arrived."[21] According to Dawson, Dewey's idea of education is almost religious, because education has to serve democracy; this is the only reason for education to exist. For Dewey, says Dawson, "democracy is not a form of government; it is a spiritual community, 'based on the participation of every human being in the formation of social values.' Thus every child is a potential member of the democratic church."[22]

Education is not indoctrination. Education is not about shaping, because the child is not clay. The child has a soul and has freedom. To educate means to help a person to be free; to fulfill himself; to realize his life; to achieve the destiny for which he was intended. Education cannot be something mechanical that we delegate in schools. "We have not been finished, and it is not clear what we have to do in order to fulfill ourselves... We are living problems, in a time that is continuously running and with an urgent need, even if because of our fault it can be disregarded."[23] Man is "aware of his incapacity to realize his own humanity. Man is powerless to be man."[24] That is why we need education.

However, any form of education implicitly defines what a human being is. Sciences study the man from different perspectives, but only anthropological philosophy studies the human being as a whole. Who is man? Although it is difficult to find a precise definition, we can state that man is the only being that can ask himself questions about his own nature. There is something inside the human being that transcends, that questions the ultimate meaning of things and of existence, and that tends to establish a relationship with the infinite. For this reason, a deep understanding of man can be achieved only through metaphysics.

The child has a body and a soul. There is no other way to explain the mystery and the unity of the person.[25] Claiming the whole nature of man, Augustine said, "We do not desire to be deprived of the body, but to be clothed with its immortality."[26] True education exists only when we do not deprive the child of his body and immortality. We have to admit that the child is a mystery.

The biggest mistake that we make in education is to deprive the child of his right to learn the mystery of reality and the mystery inside himself. Education relates to the experience of the mystery. When we deprive reality of its mystery, the person can only have perceptions of the appearance of reality, but never reality as a whole. When we deprive the person of his immortality, he can have emotions but not knowledge of the true unity and infinity of himself.

Educators need "respect for the soul as well as for the body of the child... and a sort of sacred loving attention to his mysterious identity, which is a hidden thing that no techniques can reach."[27] When we educate, are we aware of this? As educators, we should ask ourselves the following questions: "Why did you ever decide to educate another person? ... If a man is a person, with all his dignity and freedom, why do you want to say to this man how to fulfill himself?"[28] The educator is the person who activates the growth in the child. For Steiner, "to teach seriously is to lay hands on what is most vital in a human being. It is to seek access to the quick and the innermost of a child's or an adult's integrity."[29]

Education has two important aspects. First, it is about awakening ultimate questions concerning meaning as well as longings for truth, beauty, goodness, justice, and happiness. Education is about helping all those questions and longings to emerge from the inside of the person. Second, education is about helping a person enter into a relationship with an educator. Through this relationship, the person is accompanied in his goal of trying to find answers. There is true education only when the person, immersed in a human experience, encounters the answers to all those questions. The person becomes himself by using his freedom through a human dialogue, through an experience. Only then are truth, beauty, goodness, and meaning no longer simply words but rather an experience.

Giussani, in *The Risk of Education*, says the following: "As we said forty years ago, and we still haven't been able to come up with a better definition, to educate means to help the human soul enter into the totality of the real."[30] Because he defines reason as "The capacity to become aware of reality according to the totality of its factors,"[31] he affirms, "Anything less than the totality is not rationality... it is presumption, an improper expansion of what we do know, a reduction, a strangling, and the beginning of the obstruction of freedom."[32]

To educate means to help a young man discover the connection between things and the totality. If the young man does not make this connection, he is not obtaining deep knowledge about reality, because he is disregarding its most important factor: the totality, the destiny, the infinity. Therefore, he is unable to understand the universal reality because the education that he has received has been reduced to something else. Thus, it is crucial to link particular concepts with the universal.

When a student asks, "What for?" he is stopping the learning process. At that moment the educator has to suggest that it is better to ask, "What is the link between that and me?" "Why is that proposed to me?" or "What is it?" to reopen the process.[33] The educator shows the student the way he personally relates to reality. In a school, the demand for totality can be experienced through all subject areas. Therefore, the true question is, "How does this relate to the whole?" There is true education when there is a loving introduction to reality as a whole.

Training, Entertaining, or Educating

Given the importance of the word "education," it is crucial to not alter or devalue its meaning: "Recreations are not education; accomplishments are not education. Do not say, the people must be educated, when, after all, you only mean, amused, refreshed, soothed, put into good spirits and good humor, or kept from vicious excesses."[34] We often devalue education to a kind of training to get into a good college or to get a job. In that sense, people say that the goal of education is a career, success, or a degree. Other times, what we do is indoctrinate, entertain, or babysit, not educate. In other cases, we devalue education to a set of rules and a lot of information. Let us analyze some such devaluations.

During the last decades, we have valued the teaching of technical skills and the acquisition of specializations over authentic education. The most significant consequence of this has been the fragmentation of knowledge. We have broken the unity of knowledge. We have divided the tree of knowledge into a myriad of specialties and subject matters. The school is the place where we are trained to acquire certain abilities to get a good employment. We put the emphasis on the "how" instead of the "why." The goal is no longer to know reality and oneself but rather is the immediate usefulness of education and success in something, no matter what. The goal is to obtain a specific degree and a specific job. This can lead us to "a progressive animalization of the human mind and life."[35] However, the multiplication of specialties and the "animalization of our minds" make it more difficult for us to understand a global world that is affected by important problems of all different natures that are interconnected among them.

Much of the time that many students spend in middle and high school is dedicated to entertainment rather than to real learning. We arrive at this situation because there is confusion between equal opportunity and uniformity. This happens for two reasons. First, because we understand equal opportunities as "everybody has to obtain a college degree," we have to lower the standards. Thus, high school is not "high," but rather is only a continuation of the previous years. If this continues, very soon the mentality will be that "everybody has to obtain a master's degree." Therefore college, instead of university education, will become the continuation of high school too.

Second, we transmit to students the belief that a person cannot be fulfilled unless he achieves certain success in terms of academics, career, and job opportunities. I do not want to be misunderstood. I believe that it is important to provide opportunities to all in order to correct inequalities and support those who are less fortunate. However, a misconception of diversity can lead us to shape all students the same way according to a certain social ideology: we train people to become good citizens. The only alternative to this mentality is to consider the infinite value of every single young person and to accompany each one of them, through personalized paths, in his or her search for meaning. This is a more adequate approach to diversity.

Another reason why education is often devalued to a more or less dignified form of entertainment relates to the use of certain pedagogical methods and misconceptions of what comprises child-centered education. The importance of pedagogy and psychology in the classrooms has been stressed so much that we have forgotten the goal of education. We are so focused on social integration, environment interaction, students' emotions, feelings, perceptions, and reactions to stimuli that "the teacher will so perfectly succeed in knowing John that John will never succeed in knowing Mathematics."[36] According to constructivist teachers, knowledge develops naturally in children. Teachers do not have to transmit dead facts, rather they need to favor situations in which children will construct their own knowledge. When forming teachers, we put so much emphasis on certain pedagogical methods that we gradually begin to neglect the mastery in their subject matters. However, students need bricks to build. Who will provide these bricks for them? For Hirsh, constructivism is "the faith that nonacademic activities will eventuate in academic growth."[37] The result is "the substitution of doing for learning and of playing for working."[38] The purpose of child-centered education is not to entertain children or leave them alone, nor is it to transform teachers into psychologists; its purpose is to place the child in the center, transmit to him our knowledge and our experience, and acknowledge that he is a mystery in search for meaning.

We can devalue education by stressing the concept of effort, discipline, and the teaching of values. Many people emphasize the importance of inculcating values and forming the will. For them, education is about character formation, voluntarism, and ethics. However, John Locke, one of the fathers of American political principles, said, "Children are not to be taught by rules."[39] According to Locke, "None of the things they are to learn should ever be made a burden to them."[40] He believes that it is crucial to awaken a young person's desire to learn.

We teach students to develop healthy lives, to behave properly, to drive accordingly, to abide by high standards, to manage their money, and to avoid vices, and we require them to perform many service hours. They have to be serious in all aspects of life. However, we do not offer them a hypothesis about the meaning of life. Rather, it seems we oblige them to be serious about all concrete aspects of life, but not about life itself. What is life more than studies, health, or money? Life is its meaning. Unless we offer them a proposal, a hypothesis to verify, that includes the meaning of things and of life, they will not be convinced. Those values are not enough and will not last, because the young will not understand their relevance to his life's needs. The proof is that many students who receive a strong education in values during middle and high school become skeptical or vicious when they go to college. Only an education with a proposal that addresses the ultimate questions and longings of the young person can convince him.

On December 10, 1948, the General Assembly of the United Nations adopted and proclaimed the Universal Declaration of Human Rights. Article 26 states that "Education shall be directed to the full development of the human personality." The mistake that we often make is to divide the whole of the person into pieces and then try to educate some of those parts. When we educate this way, we can obtain very useful people, but according to an article that Einstein wrote in the New York Times on October 5, 1952, a man like this "with his specialized knowledge, more closely resembles a well-trained dog than a harmoniously developed person."[41] Another example of an education that trains some parts or aspects of the person is an education based on drill and practice to score well in standardized testing. In the words of Ravitch, "schools will surely be failures if students graduate knowing how to choose the right option from four bubbles on a multiple-choice test, but unprepared to lead fulfilling lives."[42] We cannot divide the unity of the person, and we cannot diminish his dignity. "Authentic education does not have its roots in knowledge, but in being."[43] Education can be education of the whole human being only when reality is considered as a whole.

Fragmentation of Knowledge

Another way to devalue the concept of education is to divide the unity of knowledge into multiple pieces. Sometimes we divide traditional subject matters, or we simply do not offer them anymore. At other times, we invent new courses. With the excuse of adapting the curriculum to the job market, providing a more child-friendly education, or attending the social demands of the youth, we transform education into a supermarket-style schooling. The student may earn credits by choosing from a huge variety and sometimes awkward or amusing array of options.

According to Hirsch, for decades, the anti-curriculum movement has succeeded in perpetuating this doctrine by requiring that all future teachers take a course on "Foundations of Education" in which "progressive child-friendly" teaching is praised, and subject-matter oriented teachers are defined as undemocratic, authoritarian, and inhumane. Professors of education have to "protect" prospective teachers from being contaminated with their old-fashioned ideas.[44] However, "Fragmented knowledge is useful only for technical purposes" and cannot "face the big challenges of our times."[45] People who are only specialists are not useful even for companies. Companies need people who not only know certain technical skills but who also know how to solve problems, how to work in teams, how to be creative, and how to understand personal and world challenges. What is at stake is that we are forming specialists in many areas without educating human beings on how to live meaningful lives.

Students accumulate large amounts of information every day through their multiple subject matters. This information is multiplied through the use of new technologies. While new technologies can be very helpful in education, they represent a great challenge. A student with his laptop or electronic tablet in class is constantly bombarded by new data and new concepts. The challenge is to discern what is fundamental and what is secondary, making the connections needed to convert that into real knowledge. Not all information is necessarily transformed into education. To accumulate information does not necessarily imply being educated. In a speech at Yale University in 1940, President Robert Hutchings said, "Our university graduates have far more information and far less understanding than in the colonial period."[46]

The result of the multiplication of disciplines and the accumulation of information is not only the destruction of important subject matters and the confusion between the essential and the secondary. The biggest problem is that we lose sight of the unity of knowledge. The student is exposed to a large variety of information and concepts that he cannot interconnect and that sometimes contradict one another. The student, left alone with so many different viewpoints, does not know how to judge things and is not able to connect the parts with the whole. Students progress from one academic year to another, but when they graduate they forget a large part of what they studied. The student can get – and also read – many different books on many different subjects, but that does not necessarily imply a good education.

"All knowledge forms a whole... for the universe in its length and breadth is so intimately knit together, that we cannot separate off portion from portion... except by a mental abstraction... sciences are the results of that mental abstraction."[47] However, the common mentality in which American schools and universities are immersed - says McIntyre – suggests that "There is no such a thing as the universe, no whole of which the subject matters studied by the various disciplines are all parts or aspects, but instead just a multifarious set of assorted subject matters."[48] I do not believe that we can reach true knowledge by omitting the study of some parts of the whole. When we break the unity of knowledge, we acquire only partial and prejudiced knowledge. All that exists forms a whole that is one subject of study. This whole includes infinite parts and facts with no natural separations in between and that have infinite relations among them. We gain knowledge when we discover the meaning of those things or relations. Sciences tell us the relations of things, they classify facts and phenomena, and they form theories that provide interpretations about relations between causes and effects.[49] For this reason, we cannot remove any important subject matter from the curriculum. If we do, we jeopardize the completeness of the rest of the disciplines and we jeopardize the learning that students obtain as a whole.[50]

We can cultivate the whole mind of the young person if we respect the unity of the tree of knowledge, which is visible throughout the curriculum. Each subject can be understood in the unity of the curriculum as a whole. Every single subject matter awakens questions for meaning in the heart of the young person. We can discover the meaning of each aspect of reality when we connect it with reality as a whole. The whole contains all parts, and each single part refers to and describes an aspect of the whole. Connecting one concept with another, the student gains real knowledge, real certainty about himself and universal reality.

The Human Dimension

In this section, we will see how crucial the human dimension is in education and how, little by little, this has lost its importance. By diminishing the importance of the human dimension in the curriculum and in the classroom, we diminish the possibility of comprehending some important aspects not only of reality, but of the human being as well, and thereby we devalue the concept of education.

Until the 18th century, we could say that the study of humanities permeated the notion that everybody had about education. During the Renaissance, Christian tradition and the tradition of the "classics" merged. The study of history, literature, philosophy, and the arts enjoyed a couple of centuries of great glory. However, a process of disarticulation of the human mentality began in the early 14th century and continued with the humanism of the Renaissance and the Enlightenment. Thus, the notion of human being suffered a process of dismemberment. The vision with which we educate our children in the 21st century has its roots in this process.

The human personality in the 14th century was wounded by the struggle of a society full of discordances such as civil wars and the ostentation of wealth in the midst of extreme poverty. People were often anguished, broken, and longing for a harmony that was difficult to find. We can see the change in mentality by comparing the verses of Dante and Petrarch. Both are very religious poets, but in Petrarch we perceive a dismembered humanity, a wounded humanity striving for unity. The disarticulation of a mentality continues in the Renaissance humanism, where the struggle towards the unity of the human person substitutes the ideal of merit for the ideal of human success. The ideal becomes the "divus," the successful man. The goal of life is to achieve success in any particular area of life. Renaissance naturalism brings another important human and ethical shift. If what the human being does is good by nature, the concept of the good is substituted with what is instinctual.[51]

We can see another big change in the concept of the human being at the beginning of the 17th century. Before this point in history, nobody openly denied the final causality of the human being. From that moment on, the human dimension became partially disregarded with the questioning of final causality. Thus, the most important part of the human being was not a matter of study, or at least a significant part of study, for some important philosophers and scientists.

Lord Francis Bacon, with his mechanist ideas, introduced a completely different vision of the human and the world at the beginning of the 17th century. According to Bacon, man can obtain the power needed to master and possess nature and the world through experimental science. Therefore, science can promote human plans to reach unlimited prosperity. He still admitted the existence of God, because he was a very religious person. He did not say that the human being does not have a final cause, but he believed that the study of final causes had been displaced: "I am moved to report not as omitted, but as misplaced," because the examination of final causes has "intercepted the severe and diligent inquiry of all real and physical causes... to the great arrest and prejudice of further discovery."[52] By dividing the study of causes into two groups, final causes with metaphysics and the rest with physics, he drew an unnatural line between science and philosophy, establishing the foundations for the rupture of the tree of knowledge.[53] However, Newton reversed Bacon's ideas, not wanting to prevent science from finding answers to ultimate questions for meaning such as the following: "Whence arises all that order and beauty which we see in the world? ... How came the bodies of animals to be contrived with so much art, and for what ends were their several parts?"[54]

In the end, Cartesianism, Empiricism, and all of the ideas of the Enlightenment, with their self-illuminated vision of the human being, provoked a decisive fragmentation of knowledge and a definitive reduction of the human dimension. This new mentality was gradually transformed into a dominant culture, in particular after the 18th century, through the influence exerted by political power and public education. This mentality can be identified with the term secularism: the assertion that man is totally autonomous, can make himself, and belongs only to himself. Secularism comes from rationalism and derives from a process of disaggregation in which the idea of man devalues not only the concept of the human being, but also the meaning of things, to whatever he decides them to be or create.[55]

This modern notion of the human being, using a diminished concept of reason, disregards the dimension of meaning in man's existence. Deep inside man we no longer find a complex of ultimate questions and longings for truth, goodness, and fulfillment. The subject of existence, the human being, is also diminished. However, the object of existence, reality, is diminished as well, and we can no longer arrive at the true meaning of reality. A man who cannot understand himself or the world does not move his freedom in pursuit of his destiny. There is no final cause and there is no destiny. Therefore, history has no meaning.

Thus, we arrive at a man reduced to biology and psychology; who very soon will be genetically modified; whose goal is utilitarian; who reduces the use of his reason and freedom; who has no destiny; who has provoked the destruction of the two world wars; who has developed atomic bombs to destroy our planet multiple times; and who uses terrorism as a way to achieve justice. Is this man more human? Does this man have a heart? Does he know what mercy is?

Modern science does not have the goal of pursuing the order and expansion of human experiences, as Neils Bohr used to say.[56] The modern scientist understands the appearance of reality, but not what is behind it. The extraordinary power of abstraction and imagination of people such as Galileo, Copernicus, Bohr, Planck, and Einstein, always striving for lawful generalizations and interconnections, always using reason in a way that could explain all factors of reality, made them discover order and beauty in the universe and regularities in the tiny particles inside matter.[57] Modern scientists very often leave behind a part of their human understanding when they try to describe reality using complex data and mathematical language.[58] Science disregards the human dimension, yet it needs it. If we want to understand reality, we need our human dimension to use all of its senses. It would be senseless to measure the level of salt inside the tears of a child if we want to understand why he is crying.[59]

It is important to cultivate the humanities, in order to understand the big problems of our times and our human condition. Philosophy is a fundamental power of interrogation that we must use to discover the meaning of reality and existence. Humanities make all sciences converge in the study and comprehension of the world and the human existence: history, philosophy, art, or literature are schools of life.[60] I would say more: we can develop the human dimension through every single subject matter by teaching the history of every discipline. In my opinion, all subject matters should teach their history so that we can see how specific men and women asked themselves questions and strove for answers; longed for beauty, justice, and fulfillment; made concrete decisions that changed the course of history; achieved great discoveries; and developed the rich culture that we have inherited. For William James, "not taught thus, literature remains grammar, art a catalogue, history a list of dates, and natural science a sheet of formulas and weights and measures."[61]

The human dimension is devalued in the teaching of almost all subject matters by disregarding the subject of study – the student – and by teaching ideas instead of facts and concrete people.[62] For example, the history of ideas does not exist. Only one history exists, which is the history of facts and individuals, the decisions that they made, and the circumstances in which they made them. The history of the American people does not exist either, only the history of concrete Americans, such as George Washington, who faced concrete circumstances and made concrete decisions. Another example of this reduction is to explain facts by providing a large amount of detailed information without awakening questions about the meaning of things in the students. Open-ended questions help students to understand the way people faced those events and to develop the skill of critical thinking. The phenomenon I am trying to illustrate through these two examples also occurs in the teaching of literature, philosophy, or the arts. Teachers usually prefer to discuss the movements of thought rather than facts, authors, and the human experience lived by those who wrote or painted their works.

Literature is often devalued to grammar and ideas. The same happens with the arts; it is devalued to techniques and currents of thought. However, literature and the arts are explosions of life and always evoke human struggles, passion, wonder, high feelings, or ultimate longings for beauty, goodness, and justice. If we cancel this dimension, novels, poems, plays, paintings, and sculptures lose their life. When students read novels or poetry, it is better not to suppress the amazement that those books – fully alive – arise in them with long, technical, or ideological lectures that, eventually, will bring them to a sure death. The students will probably forget everything but the awe that a certain passage evoked in them. In arts, for anybody with a minimum level of human sensibility, a museum is, above all, a visual banquet, due to the wonder that its works generate.

In philosophy, the reduction of the human dimension also happens when the way it is taught does not facilitate openness to the mystery behind any aspect of reality and does not awaken existential questions. In science, the reduction of the human dimension is due not only to the elimination of the teaching of its history, but also to the extreme specialization and pragmatism that its teaching suffers.

However, to educate our human dimension requires more than the teaching of humanities or the teaching of the sciences' history. True education is one that fits our humanity. This is not something automatic that happens through the use of textbooks or that we accomplish through dry information provided by certain subject matters. In education, the human dimension relates to the heart of an educator engaging the heart of a young person. The heart of every single human being is always provoked by the beauty of the arts, the human expression of literature, the drama of history, the existential questions of philosophy, the perfection of the human body, or the order and magnificence of the universe. No system of ideas and no structure of power can prevent it. No ideology and no power can eliminate the cry of the heart, which suffers the injustice, delights before beauty, and longs for meaning. Throughout history, the heart of every single man and woman of any continent, race, and culture – although manifested in different ways – expresses the same substance, the same human dimension, because the heart is the same.[63] Therefore, to learn the human dimension, we must know who the human being is.

The human being can be studied in many different sciences. We can study the relation that he has with his physical parts; we can study his brain, his mind, and his perceptions and feelings; we can analyze his relations with others; we can study the way he uses his resources and makes economic decisions; we can study his origin, his destiny, and the meaning of his existence; and we can study the relations in his community life and some other relations. Yet, if we disregard the study of one of those areas, our knowledge of the human being is diminished or distorted, and that in proportion to the significance of the area studied.[64]

Once knowledge has been fragmented, it is more difficult to understand who the human being is. We have to integrate what scientists, psychologists, sociologists, economists, historians, and other specialists say about who a man is. Philosophy used to integrate all of that knowledge, providing answers to ultimate questions, providing an understanding of human nature, and therefore facilitating the flourishing of the human.[65] However, modern man disregards philosophy and its teaching. Most high schools in the United States, public and private, do not emphasize the study of philosophy or even consider it.

Only human nature can understand the unity and the purpose of all reality. Man is the self-awareness of reality. According to Pascal, one of the greatest scientists of the 17th century:

"All bodies, the firmament, the stars, the earth and its kingdoms, are not comparable to the mind at its lowest; for the mind knows it all and knows itself; and bodies know naught of it... From all bodies together we cannot extract one little thought; it is impossible, and of a different order."[66]

Galaxies, nature, and all arts become aware of themselves in the human being. Any moment in man's life is tension towards the awareness of the whole of reality, toward the discovery of beauty, truth, and goodness. For this reason, we need educators whose humanity is the same size as our longings. The educator's humanity is this size when it awakens and engages the young person's intellect and humanity, enabling him to understand and experience the infinity and unity of his human nature.

No Education Without a Viewpoint

Any education presents a viewpoint, consciously or unconsciously. I mean a certain way of looking at reality, a certain way of seeing the world, a certain vision of life, and a certain way of doing things. There is no aseptic way of teaching science, history, economics, literature, or any other subject matter. We usually hear that education has to be neutral. With this term, we understand that it must be impartial and objective. Is that possible? For Einstein "nobody will maintain that the administration of the school and the attitude of the teachers do not have an influence."[67] Niebuhr would say that "even the most honest educator tries consciously or unconsciously to impress a particular viewpoint upon his disciples."[68]

Usually neutral and objective education means that the viewpoint is presented disguised under a fake neutralism; the viewpoint is presented unconsciously; there is indifference; or there are multiple views. In the first case, the viewpoint is an ideology that is presented in a camouflaged way under "neutral contents". In the second case, schools and teachers do not know that they have a viewpoint, or they think they are neutral when in reality they are not. In the third case, administrators and educators are indifferent and have no real interest in education. Under the excuse that they pursue neutral relationships with the students, they want to avoid relationships with them, because they do not really love them. Of course, they want to be viewed as professionals, but in reality, they want only to teach their subject and go home right after dismissal. In the fourth case, we abandon the child to a multiplicity of possibilities that he has to test spontaneously on his own. The child, lost before so many different and even contradicting views, will probably choose the most comfortable or the most instinctive. After a while, seeing that the viewpoint does not completely fulfill his humanity, he will become skeptical, not believing in any worldview; or alienated; or indifferent, not committing to anything and losing interest in his own education.

Education cannot happen without a viewpoint. In education, as with any research, a hypothesis is required. The child has to verify a hypothesis, a viewpoint. Only an educator who knows and loves the end of what he is teaching can introduce the student to the knowledge and love of that end. The clarity of the proposal is what makes teachers and students free.

We have given so much importance to the means of education that we have forgotten that there is no education without a purpose. When we do not present a worldview to our young, many of them end up involved in drugs, alcohol, random violence, mass consumption of virtual realities, and other commercial re-creations. Public schools do not serve publics; they create publics. In doing so, schools, following the vision of Jefferson, Horace Mann, and John Dewey, build the spiritual framework of the American Credo.[69]

However, parents are the ones who have the right to offer a worldview to their children. In a democratic society, schools should take into consideration the beliefs by which parents live and by which they would like their children to live as well. Schools Americanize not only children but also their parents. Glenn is very critical regarding the educational system in the United States. He believes it follows a common school agenda, which is a way to use education to conduct social reform and consists in "the deliberate effort to create in the entire youth of a nation common attitudes, loyalties, and values, and to do so under central direction by the state."[70]

The implementation of a neutral education in our schools is conducted through various means. Curriculum and textbooks are two fundamental pillars. However, the training of teachers is a more subtle and effective way, because it avoids parents and other opposing forces. Schools of education all over the country, usually under the control of progressive reformers and intellectuals, provide a particular viewpoint to all future generations of teachers, and through them, to their students.

For Glenn, the common school agenda has its roots in the French Revolution. For Rousseau, it is a fundamental mission of the State to take away from parents the education of their children, because parents are always prejudiced or ignorant, and children are born for the fatherland. In the words of Robespierre: "I am convinced of the necessity of operating a total regeneration, and, if I may express myself in this way, of creating a new people."[71] Danton, talking about the Republic of France during the revolution, believes that "it is in national schools that children must suck republican milk."[72] Republican milk is sucked through republican teachers and through republican textbooks. Some years later Guizot said, "For the advantage of progress, as well as for good order in society, a certain government of minds is always necessary."[73]

During the colonial period, before this schema could be implemented, the viewpoint offered to children in the family, at school, in the church, and in newspapers was permeated by American Puritanism through a well-articulated paideia: "a vision of life itself as deliberate cultural and ethical aspiration."[74] This vision changes depending on the cultural background, especially the predominant religious denomination of the colony. Later on, the worldview of the Founding Fathers was greatly influenced by the Enlightenment and the ideologists of the French Revolution. However, Jefferson did not succeed in the implementation of an enlightened educational system for the whole country. The enlightened ideas in our country have a different effect. They merge with the solid religious foundation of the people, creating a set of common beliefs that is offered to the new generations in the form of a viewpoint of cultural unity.

At the end of the 19th century and the beginning of the 20th century, the government took control of education and the viewpoint shifted, in great part due to the large numbers of immigrants who arrived between the time of the Civil War and the First World War. The way to continually merge thousands of people with different languages and cultures was through schools. It was the need to assimilate immigrants in the 19th century that prevented the United States from developing a religiously differentiated school system as happened at that time in European countries. Another factor was the animosity that Horace Mann and other fathers of public education had against religious schools. Thus, the common school was proclaimed the most important institution in the nation.[75] For Ravitch, public schools became "the cauldron of Americanization and assimilation... based on the popular myth that the public schools had single-handedly transformed immigrant children into achieving citizens... the school as an institution capable of individual and group salvation."[76]

Because we live in a country of immigrants, education has had greater relevance in the United States than in any other country. The common school was founded on the basis that all children had to participate and that the content of the instruction had to be imposed by the government. Thus, the worldview offered to all children was proposed by the one who controlled the power. Public schools shaped the minds of the children by transmitting the viewpoint of the power. During the Progressive era, the mission of the common school tended to broaden. Cremin says that "John Dewey called upon each school to become an embryonic social community."[77] The worldview is pragmatic and pursues more than learning, social efficiency and the establishment of a democratic community, disregarding any transcendent viewpoint or purpose.

According to Glenn, the common school was presented by Horace Mann and others in "essentially religious, salvific terms to a Protestant majority that was quite prepared to identify the institutions of American society with the Kingdom of God."[78] For him, a large proportion of Protestants in the country ceded to the nervousness provoked by immigration and believed that a civic religion for all could be accepted, in part because it kept some Christian values. In addition, Glenn believes that the promoters of the common school wanted to undermine religious schools. Joseph Chamberlain, one of the most important English politicians of the end of the 19th century and beginning of the 20th, stated in 1870 that it was the goal of his English liberal party in Europe and America "to wrest the education of the young out of the hands of the priests, to whatever denomination they might belong."[79] Also, we need to remember that during the 20th century, public education was used in many places of the world to promote horrendous viewpoints, including communism and fascism.

In the United States, the separation of Church and State – meant to guarantee religious freedom – was interpreted in a way that, in reality, did not defend religious education but rather promoted secularization. One of the points of the agenda of the common school's ideologists was to replace the religion of the people with a set of "aseptic values", which in reality constitutes a kind of "secular religion." In this sense, the common school is not secular. For Dawson, public schools favor "the pagan and secularist minority against the Christian and Jewish elements who probably represent a large majority of the population."[80]

Catholics did not accept the "secular" viewpoint offered by public education and created their own parochial system of schools. The goal was to educate children according to the vision of life and the world that their parents had. However, many Catholic schools ended up presenting a viewpoint not so different from that of the rest of schools in the country. This was due to various reasons, but in particular because the majority of their teachers were formed in the same places and with the same views held by teachers in public schools.

Nowadays, for many people the ends of education – or the "gods" that students have been asked to serve in many American schools – go from economic utility to consumerism and technology. Schools often see no contradiction between the viewpoints they offer and the viewpoint presented by commercial publicity. Schools have made information a cult, and technology is adored because it has become an end in itself. The more technology and the more information, the better, even if teachers and students often do not know how to integrate them into meaningful learning.[81]

A crucial aspect of education is its purpose, its end. When we do not know where we are going, any road will take us there. There is no education unless there is a vision of the goal. If we admit that the child has a destiny, then education needs an end, a purpose. Education is meant to help the person find his destiny but what very often happens is that we become so busy with particular aspects of education, such as finance, standards, or testing, that we forget the end of education.

When educators forget the end of education in the middle of all their commendable tests and pedagogical methods, they can make the same mistake that doctors could make when, in the midst of all their procedures, analysis, and examinations, they forget the cure of a person who could be dying. Comparing education and architecture, it makes no sense a kind of education that consists of growing in any direction without an aim, without an idea of what we are trying to build.[82]

When we affirm that "we cause ourselves to be, that we are self-made" we destroy the word destiny. "Only if there is such a thing as destiny, does the instant have any substance, any significance; only then can it be seen in function of something beyond it."[83] When we destroy the word destiny, we have to replace it with something else. We have given many examples above and we could continue mentioning others, such as usury, lust, or power – as T.S. Eliot[84] would say in the *Choruses from the Rock* – or success. Many private and public schools present the opposite view of success when they try to make students feel good regardless of their academic achievement.

The student, like any human being, has something immortal in his nature. For this reason only a viewpoint that matches his nature can satisfy him. Although a good liberal arts curriculum can be a noble instrument of education, the transcendent human nature of the child needs more. Thus, the goal of education "is not mere knowledge... rather something beyond it."[85]

If the goal of education is not the destiny of the child, we do not have the right to complain when the young are not motivated and do not commit to their learning. Only authentic beauty or truth, only real meaning can awaken a true interest in the student. Knowledge is an event, because it is the discovery of the meaning and purpose of something. The encounter with reality, presented through any aspect of education, has to be for the student the encounter with the meaning of reality, which is the encounter with his destiny. This is the goal of education.

After describing what a true education is, we have to study the notion of experience. Education has to do with experience. However, what kind of experience?

Chapter 3

Beyond Experience & Education

Education relates to the life's experience of an individual within his lived experience. For a person to discover something in reality, he has to experience it in one way or another. Therefore, to learn, the point of departure has to be the experience. If I am the one who has to acquire knowledge, then the content of the book, the suggestions of the teacher, the interpretations of other people, or other factors involved in the learning process cannot substitute something that, in the end, has to be part of my experience. However, it is not enough to state that education has to be linked to experience for one to obtain a true education. Education is more than learning by doing; it is a fully human experience. It is the journey to the infinity of reality and to the mysteries of our human existence.

In one of his latest and most mature works, *Experience & Education*, John Dewey states that "Education is a development within, by, and for experience."[86] He believes that "Education in order to accomplish its ends... must be based upon experience –which is always the actual life-experience of some individual."[87] Part of Dewey's educational philosophy is the idea that our learning correlates with experience. However, Dewey directs one of the harshest critiques to the pedagogues and reformers of the new progressive schools movement. He denounces the reduction of education to pedagogical methods and ideological battles. Dewey states that the more things change, the more they stay the same, because reformers and pedagogues "should think in terms of Education itself rather than in terms of some 'ism about education, even such 'ism as progressivism."[88]

Dewey believes that experience is not only a phenomenon, which is part of the individual's life; it is also a gradual process of gaining awareness of reality. For him, the individual has to extract "at each present time the full meaning of each present experience."[89] However, Dewey chooses to emphasize certain functional aspects, such as socialization, social experience, and the social ends of education to achieve his main goal: to integrate children in a democratic society. He emphasizes social efficiency, instead of focusing on the student and his experience of knowledge, as well as his human experience, including his longings and existential questions. It is true that American culture pervades pragmatism and hope: what is important is to improve everything to build a better future, a better society. However, the pragmatic Dewey, by disregarding the search for the truth of reality and of the human being, is failing to achieve a better future, because it is impossible to build a better reality if we do not know the meaning of the present reality. That future will be meaningless; in that future there will be no sure knowledge and no certainties.

Novak and Gowin believe that "for almost a century, students of education have suffered under the yoke of the behavioral psychologists, who see learning as synonymous with a change in behavior."[90] Some examples of changes in behavior could be the acquisition of better writing, reading, or math skills, which do not necessarily involve the acquisition of meaning. In their opinion, the most important thing is to help students pay attention to their experience so they can understand its meaning. An example could be the connection between new knowledge and previous knowledge, which enables the student to use it in future occasions. The meaning of the same experience is different for a child and for a teacher. Thus, education entails seeking the change in the meaning of experience.

It is true that in the 20th century there have been many well intentioned attempts to put the child at the center of the educational process, promoting the research of student learning, inquiry, discovery, and the study of the cognitive process. However, the pragmatic mentality of those researchers and reformers led them to overemphasize pedagogy, methodology, psychology, technology, tools to use, and other functional factors, subordinating the subject, who is the center of the educational process, and diminishing the concept of experience.

For Dewey education requires experience.[91] But in education, how deep can we go in the study of experience: only to the functional aspects of knowledge, or further?[92] If the answer is "further", then it is necessary to establish the boundaries of experience. However, who will do it, and what criterion will be used?[93] What is crucial is a true understanding of the term "experience". The problem is that we take for granted that we have it. We should not reduce the understanding of experience to empirical perceptions.

We often distort experience or reduce it to feelings, prejudices, or partial interpretations without any support from objective truth. We should open our understanding of the term experience to the human experience as a whole.

Two of the main reductions of experience come either from the philosophy of Descartes and Kant or from empiricism. Let's study the first one following Di Martino.[94] Descartes uses doubt not to destroy knowledge but to find justifiable knowledge. For him, reality is its representation; the mental representation of things grants their existence. The problem is that the internal processes in the intellect of the individual acquire a certainty of their own. For Kant, the subject constitutes objects through the data of experience. Kant believes that there is no knowledge without experience, but, agreeing with Descartes, he states that experience is subjective and is a limited realm whose boundaries are predetermined by the intellect and the sensible perceptions. In what way does this interpretation reduce experience? The reduction is produced, says Di Martino, when the capacity of reality to manifest itself as a phenomenon is limited to a type of cognitive capability that is developed following the mechanical philosophy of social sciences. This way, the manifestation of reality as given, as superabundance of "the given and givenness," is turned into a constitutive dimension, a created dimension with its own laws. This happens because of the claim that the subject precedes and influences that manifestation. Thus, knowledge is no longer a disclosure, unveiling, or discovery of contents with an original autonomous configuration that comes before any definition; rather, it is something constructed.

The second reduction, derived from empiricism, is the reduction of experience to a random and blind multiplication of senseless perceptions that are interpreted by some capacity of our mind. This way the experience of reality is limited to a disorganized conglomerate of empirical stuff.[95] This second reduction can be perceived if we follow how in the 13th century, Roger Bacon used to differentiate the concept of experience, experiment, and experimental science. He states that experience is not only a collection of facts but also a way to discover the causes of those facts. In his opinion, experience provides not only data to verify conclusions but also data to develop explanations of reality. According to Roger Bacon, experience has a broad meaning and includes three different senses: intuition, understood as a clear vision of things, along with interior perceptions or "illuminations"; observation of phenomenon and their causes; and technological applications.[96]

Modern science usually reduces experience. The fact that the questions that scientists put to nature are answered in mathematical patterns and that the observer influences the phenomenon observed imply that no model can provide the right explanation of reality. Some models may work in our minds or in a virtually controlled nature but they fail to provide a universal explanation of our experience of reality. The big problem of the incapacity of modern science to represent the sensual world is that when we cancel the reality that we perceive with our senses, we are canceling the transcendent world too. Therefore, this reductive use of reason encloses us in the prison of our mind and does not allow us to conceptualize our world. We will remain imprisoned, if we continue assuming that reality cannot reveal itself to the human being.[97]

A concept of reason disconnected from the real world cannot explain the world. According to Jean Guitton, "a reasonable man is one who submits reason to experience."[98] If we submit reason to experience, reason has the capacity to enter into a relationship with reality, to understand reality. Scientific experience is based on the human desire to understand reality. Precisely because we understand some parts of reality, reality invites us constantly to discover more, to discover its meaning; but there is always a mystery in our experience of reality.

This mystery presents itself in our experience through ultimate longings for truth, justice, and fulfillment as well as through ultimate questions: what is our origin and destiny? Why is life worth living? What is the meaning of life and death?[99] Some unreasonable positions try to either empty those questions or reduce them. They are unreasonable because they try to explain reality and those questions without taking into account all of the factors involved in them. The first one is the theoretical denial of the questions, affirming that they make no sense. Second, the voluntary substitution of questions happens when the energy of those questions is substituted by willpower, in the form of personal praxis, utopianism, or a social project. Third, the practical denial of the questions happens when the individual develops his life trying to keep the questions from surfacing.[100]

There are three other unreasonable positions in which the questions are reduced. First, the sentimental evasion deals with the attitude in which the individual expresses feelings related to the questions, but there is no real search for an answer. Second, the desperate negation completely denies the possibility of an answer to the questions. Third, alienation considers ultimate questions only as stimuli to collaborate in the edification of progress towards the future. This position is unreasonable because people are alienated by those who control the power and establish what progress means.[101]

The pedagogy of John Dewey, which has influenced education greatly in America and the Western world during the last century, falls into the first category of positions emptying ultimate questions. Dewey believes that "to abandon the pursuit of reality and the search for absolute and immutable value can seem like a sacrifice. But this renunciation is the condition of entering upon a vocation of greater vitality,"[102] which is to look for values accepted by the majority to achieve social efficiency and a democratic society.

However, it is crucial that ultimate questions not be avoided by cancelling a part of our experience, because if we cancel it, we cancel part of reality. If we have a prejudice against ultimate questions or ultimate causes, we can develop logic or scientific models or theories of reality, but those models will never explain the integral experience of reality that we have, which includes the mystery of reality. Reason, because it is compelled to understand our experience of existence, "is forced by its very nature to admit the existence of something incomprehensible."[103] According to Einstein, "the most beautiful experience we can have is the mysterious."[104] Sooner or later the intuition is awakened in the human being that maybe there is something beyond himself, a reality that can provide an explanation to that mystery.

If we have such high needs, feelings, and questions, there must be an answer to them. Therefore, we have to admit the possibility that this mystery, this final causality, reveals itself to us. "The fundamental dogma of the Enlightenment is the impossibility of a revelation... extreme attempt that reason makes in order to dictate by itself the measure of the real, and, therefore, the measure of the possible and impossible in reality."[105] Einstein, not reducing his reason and not reducing his experience of reality states that "the scientist is possessed by the sense of universal causation."[106]

Knowledge is the event of the encounter of two factors: human energy and reality, understood as something given, objective, a presence. In our experience, reality does not form or make itself, but it makes itself evident. Experience is reality becoming evident; it is the revelation of something that was already there. Modern telescopes can bring very near to us stars that did not exist for serious scientists some centuries ago. How can they bring into existence something so far away? They can do it if that faraway reality enters into experience. Therefore, in experience, reality and truth become recognizable. What originates as experience and what determines the boundaries of experience is givenness, donation; it is reality as something given.[107]

According to the phenomenological approach of Husserl and Heidegger, if our point of departure for any research is reality, this means the point of departure is experience.[108] Knowledge depends on donation. "Givenness always determines knowledge and not the inverse."[109] The event is something unexpected, the irruption of something from outside of us. The event is a fact in which the mystery hidden inside an object reveals itself to us through experience. Through an event, reality becomes transparent and we understand a little piece of the world. For Einstein, "the fact that (the world) is comprehensible is a miracle."[110]

In the words of Heisenberg, one of the founders of quantum mechanics and author of the Uncertainty Principle, we can see how reality and meaning happen unexpectedly in our experience as something given. He describes his surprise when he discovered that atomic theory is based on simple internal relations:

"The whole area of internal relations in atomic theory is unexpectedly and clearly spread out before my eyes... in all their mathematic abstraction, and incredible degree of simplicity, is a gift... In fact these relations cannot have been invented: they have existed since the creation of the world."[111]

Now that we have clarified the boundaries and the origin of experience, we will connect the concept of experience with the concept of education. "Experience means to live what causes me to grow. A person grows as a result of experience."[112] It is through experience that nature facilitates the growth of the person. Thus, experience involves the awareness of growing in it. We grow only when we are helped by something that is outside of ourselves, by something objective that we encounter.

What is important is to connect experience with meaning. For Giussani, "What characterizes experience is our understanding something, discovering its meaning. To have an experience means to comprehend the meaning of something. This is done by discovering its link to everything else; thus experience means also to discover the purpose of a given thing and its function in the world."[113] The term "meaning" is the translation of the Italian word "senso", which also means direction. We do not grow in a random direction. Meaning is a direction to follow in our search, in our inquiry, in our discovery of the world. Meaning entails not only moving in a direction but also includes our capacity to make connections while we proceed in that direction.

One of the key aspects of education is this capacity to make connections. For John Dewey, an individual develops an integrated personality "only when successive experiences are integrated with one another."[114] We digest what we receive when we see the meaning of each thing; when we see the interdependence of things; when we view things as a whole; when the whole enters and permeates every single thing and assigns to each one of them a meaning.[115] We discover truth when, in our experience, we discover links between the meaning of specific things and the whole.

But, how do we make those connections? Dewey states "Judgment puts together what is observed."[116] There is no experience if we make only mechanical connections with reality, because what it is needed is a capacity for evaluating. Experience is more than trying something; it "coincides with a judgment we make about what we try... what defines experience is understanding something, discovering its meaning."[117] We prove this statement when we see people who have accumulated many years of experience but lack certainty and do not even understand their lives. After graduation in high school and college, a student has attended hundreds of classes and has read hundreds of books. However, this is not enough, because if such things are not adequately judged, the student is unable to make connections among them and either does not remember much of them or is confused in the midst of multiple opinions. This is the reason so many students obtain degrees and diplomas but are not engaged in what they are learning, are passive or skeptical, or, simply, do not understand their lives and the world. If the criterion of judgment is a cloud of contradicting and subjective interpretations, we are confused or enslaved by them, as usually happens with the powerful influence of the media.

The criterion that permits us to judge is inside us, given to us as part of our nature. Giussani calls it "elementary experience." It is a complex of original evidences and needs – such as the need for truth, fulfillment, and justice – which spark the human motor and with which we compare every reality that we encounter and everything that happens in our lives. For him, knowledge happens when an instant comparison, an instant judgment, is made between that human energy – with the form of original needs – and the reality encountered. He believes that this evaluation that we conduct is not subjective – therefore knowledge is not subjective – because the criterion is objective; it emerges from within the structure at the origin of the person. Everybody has it, and it is the same for every single human being. The judgment that I obtain could be wrong, because I can apply the criterion incorrectly – the same thing happens if I incorrectly apply any scientific method – but the criterion is objective.[118]

I have to compare what I see, what I read, what is discussed in class, with my elementary experience. Others' interpretations and opinions, be it a teacher or a book, can help, but they cannot substitute for work that must be done only by me, because I only acquire knowledge if it is part of my experience. That is why it is so important for teachers not to close questions by giving quick answers to their students. It is very important to leave them open so that the student can discover the answer in his experience. This is particularly important when we are dealing with ultimate questions and final causes.

When this human energy, this complex of needs, encounters the meaning of a given reality, the human being perceives a correspondence. "Truth is an adequatio rei et intellectus, a correspondence between the object and self-consciousness."[119] In other words, a correspondence is experienced between the meaning of that reality and the meaning of our existence.[120] Education involves a comparison between what we see and the ultimate meaning of everything. When correspondence happens, we experience a moment of epiphany, a moment of sudden intuitive understanding, a flash of insight, an event.

Experience has not only a cognitive aspect but also an affective and relational element. The more urgency we have to discover the meaning of things, the more reality attracts us and the more we are compelled to experience it. Experience happens in relation with reality, in relation with what makes reality exist. Also, experience can be activated by another experience. The educator's experience activates the student's experience. This can happen when the educator understands reality. If the educator witnesses how reality in his experience becomes evident and transparent, then he can transmit what he has witnessed. This event awakens the student's desire to live the same thing, to live the experience that the educator lives. Also, affection received by the student activates his interest in himself and in reality; therefore, it activates his experience of himself and reality. In our relationships with another, we discover the world and ourselves.

A true experience of education is shown on the horizon of the relationship between the educators and the young person. A dialogue in the *Divine Comedy* between Dante and Ser Brunetto, his teacher, provides an example of this experience: "For in my mind is fixed, and touches now my heart the dear and good paternal image of you, when in the world from hour to hour taught me how a man becomes eternal."[121] It is fundamental that every human being experience this mysterious sense of greatness and humility, this sense of becoming fulfilled and being aware that we have a place in eternity. "To educate means to help the human soul enter into the totality of the real... to help someone understand the elements of reality in their fruitful multiplying, up to a totality which is always the true horizon of our actions."[122] Education is openness to the totality, to the ultimate meaning of everything. Education is far more than learning by doing; it is a human experience in which the person grows in self-awareness, awareness of particular realities, and awareness of reality as a whole.

Chapter 4

A Method that Works

Many people may have a vision of education similar to the one described in the previous chapters. Many people may want to implement a similar vision of education to overcome the human crisis in which we are immersed and face the challenges of the 21st century. However, the problem is how to implement that vision. If we inspire people with a venture but then are unable to put it into effect, everybody ends up frustrated. This is why a method is needed. What kind of method? A method centered on the integral experience of the person. Such experience cannot be taught in a course; it must be lived. It is a life experience within a lived experience.

We can find suggestions for this method in *The Risk of Education* by Giussani. In his opinion, "Education means to develop all the structures of an individual until they are complete, while at the same time affirming all the possible active links those structures have to reality."[123] A well-rounded educational vision can provide a good academic program; can achieve certain social, ethical, cultural, civic, or behavioral goals; and can provide health education, sports, and extracurricular activities, but above all, it has to develop all structures of the human person and his links with reality.

Educational plans usually aim at graduation or at a particular aspect of reality but not at the humanity of the person or at reality as a whole. We can teach without educating, and students can continue learning until the day of their graduation without becoming educated.[124] The young person, especially during adolescence, becomes aware of himself and of the world in which he lives. An adequate educational method has to provide a sort of explanatory hypothesis. This method must introduce the young person to an adequate relationship with things that allows those things to present themselves and reveal their meaning to him. With a hypothesis of meaning, the person can experience knowledge and comprehend nature, the universe, physical forces, facts, history, material and immaterial elements, and truths.

Carron says, "For many years people thought that it was enough to teach students mathematics or language, instead of suggesting the way to enter into reality. This fact has generated a terrible indifference, an incapacity to be interested in anything."[125] Just as it would be inhuman to give a toy to a child without giving him the instructions for its use, "it is inhuman to bring a child to the world without giving him the instructions for use – i.e. without introducing him to reality."[126]

This method is not the imposition of a set of ideas but rather is a working hypothesis suggested to the young person to help him understand his own experience and discover how pertinent his journey of knowledge is to his life's needs. Giussani tells us that on the first day of school, he always said the following to his students: "I'm not here so that you can take my ideas as your own; I'm here to teach you a true method that you can use to judge the things I will tell you. And what I have to tell you is the result of a long experience."[127]

In this method, the educator transmits a hypothesis of meaning to the student and invites him to verify it. The educator awakens in the student something that is inside him: the desire for knowledge, truth, beauty, and fulfillment. The educator illumines his reason and activates his freedom so that he can test the hypothesis, grow as a man, and develop a journey to the truth. The goal is to empower the student, so that he, only through this method, becomes able to recognize truth by himself. Thus, the student sees how the world rises to his awareness, and reality becomes transparent in his own experience.

The method could be described with seven words: the journey to truth is an experience. Important aspects of this method are experience, freedom and affection, reality as the sign of something more, and knowledge and truth as an event. Let us summarize the main elements of this method. The first one is a proposal, a hypothesis of meaning with which the student can obtain certainties about the way the world works. The second one is the educator. The presence of an educator is meant to embody and transmit the proposal and to activate the commitment of the young person in the verification of the hypothesis. The third one is the student. The student uses his freedom and reason to test the proposal. The environment and the community – other fundamental elements – are the places where the student verifies the proposal.[128] Now one by one, let us study the elements of this method.

A Culture Is Transmitted: The Proposal

The point of departure of our journey, the first element of the method, is a proposal made to the young person. What is the proposal, and who chooses it? In a totalitarian regime the government chooses the hypothesis of meaning, the proposal to be made to all children of the country. In a democratic society, it does not work that way. The content of the proposal is the culture, the tradition in which the child has been born. Culture, society, and history are based on the knowledge of reality of the people who lived before us. If we do not recognize this type of knowledge, we destroy all human culture. Einstein portrays this concept very well when, addressing a group of children, he said: "The wonderful things you learn in your schools are the work of many generations... All this is put into your hands as your inheritance in order that you may receive it, honor it, add to it, and one day faithfully hand it on to your children."[129] However, the proposal cannot be the transmission of a package of information with a mere description of things and their mechanics; it also must include two things: meaning and lived experience.

Parents pass on to their children a certain view of things. Schools and teachers help parents in passing on to their children a worldview. Tradition is "the whole structure of values and meanings into which a child is born... the adolescent uses tradition as a sort of explanatory hypothesis."[130] The adolescent uses this hypothesis of meaning to compare everything. The hypothesis provides the possibility of acquiring certainties, of discovering that things have a meaning, and of facing life and any challenge or problem with the hope that there will be an answer.

At the same time, the proposal cannot tie the teacher and the student to the past. It has to be lived in the present; it has to facilitate a place where it can be experienced. From within a life experience that speaks for itself, a working hypothesis of how the world works is proposed by the educator to the freedom of the young person. This life experience has to show the correspondence of the hypothesis with the person's needs.[131] The proposal must address something that is already awakened in the person; otherwise, the proposal does not make sense to the individual. As Niebuhr says, "Nothing is so incredible as an answer to an unasked question."[132] The young person sees how the proposal works because he acquires meaning and because the proposal matches his life's needs. The proposal cannot be reduced to an intellectual exercise. It implies a life, a promise, an invitation to follow an experience. The young person follows the invitation because the proposal has set him into motion. He follows with the desire to live that experience with the person who is proposing it.

We said before that the human being and his destiny are a mystery. In the experience of every human being there are longings for truth, justice, fulfillment, beauty, and goodness. The child, at least once in his life, has lived something true, good, or beautiful and would like to live it again. His heart burns with ultimate questions about the meaning of life and of things. He has probably seen the pain or death of a relative or friend. His curiosity and desire to find an answer cannot be pushed aside. For this reason, the proposal must address the deepest needs and questions of the young person. The working hypothesis must show an experience that educates his humanity by addressing those needs and questions.

For our proposal, what tradition should we use? Obviously, the one the child has been born into and has grown up with. The American culture has been influenced by various traditions, but above all, it is part of the Jewish-Christian-Greek-Roman tradition that started more than two thousand years ago and is the fruit of the history of the Jewish people, ancient Greece, the Roman Empire, the Christian tradition, and the whole of Western civilization. There is no tradition like this one. Dawson argues, "It is distinguished from that of all the great oriental cultures by the fact that it was not confined to a priestly caste, or to the study of a sacred tradition, but formed an integral part of the life of the community."[133] As Edward Eggleston describes, there was a transit of civilization from England to America during the 17th century. Cremin acknowledges, "insofar as the colonists transplanted the English village community to America, they transplanted an educational configuration of household, church, and school."[134] The process is complex; this culture evolved in a particular way, and there were other transits of civilizations, but it is true that Christianity and the Western civilization shaped the country. The view of democracy, liberty, justice, and solidarity that we have in our country comes from this tradition, not from nihilism or oriental religions, which are now very popular among many teachers in America.

There are educators who reject the idea of providing a working hypothesis to the child, affirming that it is better to allow him to grow abandoned to a spontaneous evolution with no guidelines. Education needs socialization, but it is far more than that. For Hirsch:

> "The new kind of teaching espoused by Rousseau and Dewey, which avoids rote learning and encourages the natural development of the child on analogy with the development of an acorn into an oak... has its drawbacks, one of which is that a child is not in fact like an acorn. Left to itself, a child will not grow into a thriving creature; Tarzan is pure fantasy. To thrive, a child needs to learn the traditions of the particular human society and culture it is born into."[135]

The child has been born into a world that existed before him and will continue existing after him, but the child is not a plant or a dog. The child needs to understand the world because the human being is the self-awareness of the world. To abandon the child to autonomous and spontaneous growth "blocks the young personality that is in the process of being formed and throws it off balance."[136] A self-educated child bombarded by contradicting opinions and hypotheses inevitably is led to skepticism, passivity, and uncertainty. The child will embrace the most instinctively seductive proposal.[137] An initial hypothesis is needed as a point of departure, even if the child later decides to discard it. We should not complain about the behavior or passivity of the youth if we did not give them a hypothesis of meaning.

The Educator

Tradition gives to the child an authority, the educator. The etymology of *auctoritas*, or "authority", underlines how important the role of the educator is in education. Auctoritas comes from the latin verb "augere", which means "to make grow". The authority is the person – parent, teacher, adult – who activates the growth and the fulfillment of the child. The authority suggests the working hypothesis to the young person. The educator is the physical location and the expression of the hypothesis. Education is not a partial activity but rather a dimension of life. Therefore, the authority personally and concretely shows that it is possible to be completely fulfilled because he lives what he is proposing. The authority incarnates the truth of the young person, because the truth is not an idea; it is a living and personal reality.[138]

The truth of reality and the truth of the young person cannot be an abstract horizon, a vision imagined in a strategic planning, or the result of the implementation of educational programs. This truth is a life experience. The horizon lies before the departure of the educational process. It dwells in the person of the educator.[139] The authority shows this experience through the way he lives; through the way he sees reality and judges things. The presence of the authority shines and captivates because of the unity of his life. The beauty of that life experience awakens the desire in the young person to follow it.

An important aspect of the role of the educator is coherence. However, it is more important to emphasize the concept of ideal coherence than moral coherence. In the *Divine Comedy*, the lack of moral coherence of Ser Brunetto – Dante's teacher, who is in hell – did not prevent him from educating Dante.[140] Ideal coherence is a constant reminder of the proposal, a stable standard for judging everything, and a stable commitment to guarantee the link between the student's inconsistent freedom and the ultimate meaning of reality.[141]

Every educator, through the way he lives, acts, and judges things, proposes a hypothesis. The proposal can be nihilism and relativism, a set of "aseptic" and empty values, a distant relationship that lacks any human dimension or entertainment. In the end, very often the goal can be either to equip the student with information and skills that enable him to go to college, or to isolate him, with the belief that he will make it on his own. In these cases, the authority becomes almost useless, because he does not help the young person grow. The result often is either no growth or anarchical and irrational growth.[142]

Many educators are happy discharging the burden of their responsibilities for the children they brought into this world or for the children they have in their classrooms. Children are accomplices in this game when they try to disregard every authority as though they were oppressed by them. Educators and children often understand authority in terms of absolute superiority with an expiration time: for parents, it is as long as their children are minors; and for teachers, it is as long as the children are their students. This understanding is not human and is quite contradictory if we take into account that the relationship of educator-child is not temporary by nature.[143]

There are educators who destroy souls.[144] Some educators engage the young person out of selfishness for reasons such as the desire to impose certain ideas, the desire to have followers, money, or personal affirmation, or because of a lack of affection.[145] On many occasions, the result of the educational process is only vain sentimentality. What empowers a man or a woman to teach another human being? Where lies the wellspring of authority?[146] The only answer is total gratuity. The only motivation is true love. The wellspring of authority is not a college degree but rather a certain life experience. Only those who are constantly educated and are truly committed to the truth of their own lives can commit to the lives of others.[147] The responsibility for a child is paternity; to conceive oneself in the function of the other. The wellspring of authority is "a sense of detachment and respect. It is a sense of fear and trembling in front of the mystery that dwells in the students, whose life is both yours and not yours."[148]

Knowledge of reality is acquired through a witness. The educator, as John Locke reminds us, "should know the world well... and he should be able to show to his pupil... what lies at the bottom... the world as really it is, before he comes wholly into it."[149] We discover who is a true authority when we see a person who witnesses a full awareness of reality and a fulfilled humanity: through the way he uses reason; through the way he teaches a subject matter; through the way he awakens questions for meaning in the children; through the depth and stability of the relations that he develops; and through the way he is.

The authority shows that reality is positive and it is a sign, an arrow that points to something else.[150] We gain this experience when we see an educator moved by reading a certain passage in a novel or a poem; showing the harmony of the cosmos; discussing the beauty of nature or the perfection of the human body; explaining the mystery hidden behind mathematic problems; showing the mystery of matter and its tiny particles; amazed by the beauty of a piece of art; moved by some facts of history or by a piece of music. This educator awakens our ultimate questions and needs. Only one who is like this, only one who is moved, can move others. Thus, the witness develops the self-awareness of the child.[151] We see a victory and a certainty in the face of an educator, in the way he lives and acts, and we want that for our own lives. The encounter with such a person awakens interest and respect and is followed.

The educator suggests the proposal by communicating himself, by revealing himself, by exposing himself. It is impossible to introduce an individual to reality as a whole without proposing its meaning. The proposal is not a discourse; rather it is an invitation to a human relationship. It carries the drive originating from the presence of the educator, a drive with a promise inside. The communication of the adult is a risk, because it is abandoned to the fragile freedom of the young. Thus, the educator needs humility and certainty to awaken the desire for beauty and truth in the young. His invitation is to a journey of knowledge in which the child will grow as a man. For this, the educator needs patience, because he has to be aware that time is the place where the truth of reality manifests itself.

The Young Tests the Proposal

The adolescent verifies the proposal in his experience. He tests the truth of the working hypothesis. The most important aspect of education is not to say or transmit a proposal but to assist the teenager in this verification, to help him understand what it is said or proposed. This is how the adolescent takes ownership of the knowledge discovered, acquires his convictions and his certainties. The goal is not to make children believe what educators say but rather to help them verify whether what is valid for educators is also valid for them. Conviction is born when the young person sees the truth of the working hypothesis in his experience, when he sees that the hypothesis is pertinent to his life's needs.

Critical thinking is a crucial aspect of this method. There is no education without criticism. Critique and criticism come from the Greek term "krisis". This word is also linked to the term "problem". The proposal moves the young and activates his critical thinking: he has a "problem" before him. Giussani uses the image of a knapsack to explain this process. Those who love their children have put in their children's knapsacks the best decisions and experiences that they made. Until children are in third grade, they believe whatever their parents and teachers tell them. At a certain age – usually in fourth and fifth grade and middle school – children critically examine the content of the knapsack: "Is this true?" The standard for judgment is the same as the one discussed in the chapter dedicated to experience; it is that inner complex of needs for truth, love, goodness, and fulfillment, which is common to everybody and comes with our nature as human beings. When the young examine the knapsack, they will see whether its contents are true, false, or inconclusive; they will see whether the hypothesis works, if it corresponds. Following this process the adolescent will grow. However, criticism does not consist in doubting everything – as we hear very often – or in agreeing without reasons. It consists of becoming aware of the proposal received. Criticism means finding the reasons for the reality and tradition in which we live, discovering a new truth and a new good in our own experience. Without this process, the child does not mature and is like a leaf tossed by the wind from one place to another, victim and slave of the strongest wind, usually the media.[152]

It is reasonable for the teenager to adhere to a proposal when it corresponds to his deepest needs and longings. Otherwise, the proposal should be rejected. Conviction is born when the youth finds the link between the working hypothesis and his life's needs.[153] An example of this correspondence can be seen in a moment in which we perceive the meaning of the mystery behind an aspect of reality or a fact studied. If we perceive that this reality is the sign of something else, then we are led to the intuition of the truth of that reality. To perceive that link and to have that intuition matches our need for truth. This dynamic is similar to the one that a child follows when he is solving a mathematical problem. When the person perceives the meaning of that mystery – in the case of the mathematical problem, when the child intuits the solution – correspondence is experienced, and it is accompanied by an increase in fulfillment. Following this method, we are able to explore and embrace – at least at the level of intuition – any reality.

This verification has three premises. The first is realism: The starting point for the test of the proposal is reality, not our ideas. We have to pay attention to ourselves in action and then compare the proposal with our experience. The second one is reasonableness: love for rationality. The third premise is the morality of knowledge: to love truth more than we love ourselves.[154]

To test the proposal, the youth needs to use his intelligence and freedom in terms of the commitment of his will. Both reason and freedom are played at the same time and cannot be dissociated. First, we will discuss how reason is employed during the test of the proposal, and then we will discuss freedom.

Reason is needed to confirm the truth of what is tested, especially when correspondence comes and goes. It is important to educate our concept of reason. Reason uses different procedures in coming to the place of knowing, because the object imposes the method of knowledge. If I want to inhale the aroma of a great wine, I bring the glass to my nose, not my ear. That is why to know chemical reactions, we do not use a trigonometric demonstration but rather a chemical procedure; and to know existential realities, we cannot use the mathematical method. Reason is the human capacity to grasp the meaning of reality according to all of its factors.[155]

However, reason cannot be separated from human experience and all the factors that experience involve, such as feelings, longings, and freedom. Scientific reason tries to eliminate these factors, but it is impossible to do so. Reason works only as part of human experience. In the process of verification, there are positive and negative feelings involved. We said before that knowledge is an event and is grasped in a moment of epiphany. When we realize that we grasped the meaning of something, then we experience "felt significance". This feeling is more or less acute, depending on the depth of the new concept or link grasped.[156] Feelings such as boredom, anguish, fear, or joy cannot be eliminated and are part of the verification, but they have to be appropriately understood and put in the proper place.[157] The verification of existential truths involves pain in the process, but also epiphany and fulfillment.

The second element needed in the process of verification is freedom. When the educator proposes the hypothesis, the youth has to use his freedom to test it. Unless the youth is personally and consciously committed to this process he cannot experience truth, because a person can understand a reality only if he is in it. Certainty arises when the youth spends time becoming familiar with that reality. When an educational method dissociates reason and freedom – for example, by appealing to abstract responsibility or shallow curiosity – then it is impossible to acquire certainties.[158] The student has to decide and commit in order to know. Furthermore, the event of knowledge shows itself to those who in an active way are experiencing it: the more truth is revealed, the more truth is called forth.[159]

Freedom is not the ability to choose among many options, an abstract combination of will and intelligence, or a mechanical answer to a stimulus. Cervantes in *Don Quixote* defines it:

> "Freedom, Sancho, is one of the most precious gifts that heaven has bestowed upon men; no treasures that the earth holds buried or the sea conceals can compare with it; for freedom, as for honor, life may and should be ventured; and on the other hand, captivity is the greatest evil that can fall to the lot of man."[160]

Freedom is the experience of a risk, the risk needed to adhere to what is proposed. The student experiences risk when the proposal provokes him, calls him forth. Many times the student has reasons for recognizing a truth, but they are abstract, they are not part of his experience. Because they are abstract, they do not move his will. Thus, the youth sees the reasons, but he does not move; he lacks the energy needed to detach himself from passivity or from his preconceptions shaped by the dominant mentality. The youth does not adhere to the truth because there is a gap between his reason and his will. This phenomenon can be described with the image of a rope-climbing event. The guide can ask you to jump, but panic prevents you from jumping.[161] Verification implies a risk, which is why the educational process depends on the quicksand of the youth's freedom.[162]

The presence of the educator is crucial when the adolescent struggles in the process of verification. Even Dewey believes that "guidance given by the teacher to the exercise of the pupil's intelligence is an aid to freedom, not a restriction upon it."[163] A dialogue must happen in which teacher and student play their freedoms completely. The relationship between teacher and student is an exchange of trust and love. If one of the two does not commit his freedom, then there is no educational experience. And the opposite is also true: in a true verification the past and tradition become something present with new developments. When this happens, the teacher also learns from the student.[164]

Some people believe that it is good to substitute the relationship of teacher-student with new technologies as much as possible. I believe that new technologies can greatly enhance learning but that the knowledge of reality cannot be devalued to an abstract search or to a drill of exercises before a computer. Truth reveals itself in the experience of an educative dialogue. For example, a teacher can ask his student what an object is. The student can answer by saying that it is a small black box, with a screen and buttons and chips inside. However, the description of all of its parts does not provide a meaning. At that point, it is important that the teacher, in this dialogue, affirm the meaning of the object: it is a smartphone. Presenting the meaning to the student, the teacher is opening a horizon. This is especially important when existential concepts are involved. With these concepts, everybody can give quick answers and close the questions, but only true educators raise ultimate questions and open horizons of meaning.

The educator must respect the youth's freedom. This is especially difficult for parents and teachers. Educators can be vampires of souls; they can physically and psychologically destroy their pupils. Pupils can ruin their educators as well.[165] The educator has to pay attention to any reaction that the proposal may provoke in the youth and correct him with love if there is a need to do so. The etymology of "to correct" comes from the Latin "corrigere," which means, "to hold together."[166] The youth is held together by the love of the adult; the young is supported in his process of verification. What is important is that the educator maintains the same method. The child has to use his freedom and reason and has to see in his experience that a proposal works; and he has to acquire knowledge through the event of the manifestation of reality. Impatience cannot force the adult to find shortcuts, because this will distort the educational process. Therefore, the educator has to be patient, remembering first that freedom always implies the youth's creativity, and second, that the youth and his freedom are very often weak; freedom matures with the growth of the youth.

Environment and Community

In the environment, the individual develops objective relationships. Therefore, it is in those relationships where he has to see that the hypothesis of meaning works, especially in the family, in the school, and with his friends. The environment is the place where the proposal is tested and experience takes place. Given the overwhelming influence of media and peer pressure on the youth, it is crucial for him to see the validity of the proposal in his own world.[167] This is how certainty grows in the adolescent and enables him to face any situation.

The proposal is not tested in the abstract, but rather in a place, in a community. In the educational experience, there is a personal dimension and a dimension of community. The school is an extension of the community life that the child lives in his family. Relationships are part of the human nature. Man lives and is fulfilled in his relationships with others, in a community. For this reason, the proposal has to be verified in action within a lived reality. It has to be something that we personally experience in a living place. Education is an involvement in a communal event. The community is not a group where individuals are gathered but rather a life shared together with a certain approach to everything: studies, family, friendship, love, and so forth.[168]

The educational experience does not happen in our imagination but in reality. This is why classrooms, tables, and chairs are needed in education buildings. Furthermore, the student does not make the journey alone but with educators and peers. In this pathway, he finds companions, people with similar needs and experiences. The problem is that the individual does not choose these companions, and if he wants to make the journey, he has to allow them to be part of his life. Moreover, in education it is very important to acquire knowledge through the eyes of others. For this reason, an important element of the journey is the communitarian phenomenon.

The use of free time has particular importance in the verification because it is during this time that the person's choices are manifested. A true educational proposal is able to attract the interest of the student even during his free time. Unfortunately, what very often happens is that extracurricular activities are reduced to entertainment and constitute a distraction from the educational proposal. We need to remember that the youth clearly embodies the proposal when he lives it during his free time.[169]

The human being is free, but his nature is wounded; sometimes he does what he does not want to do, and at other times, he does not do what he wants to do. For this reason, the adolescent needs help in his journey. In addition to the educator, the youth needs the community for complete development of his freedom because he overcomes fear and risk through the communitarian phenomenon. Through community, the experience of risk becomes an experience in which freedom is fulfilled. At the same time, the community does not substitute freedom and personal decision.

How does the student obtain the energy needed in order to commit to the verification of the proposal? The answer is in a life experience. The proposal does not have only an intellectual or cultural dimension but also a dimension of charity and love. The hypothesis of meaning received is tested and shared with others. A youth, who is convinced after testing a proposal, embodies the proposal and shares it with others. For example, if a student likes a chemistry project assigned by a teacher and developed during a particular week, the student is more attentive in class during that week, studies more chemistry, and wants to share his work with his peers.

Students living and sharing a life experience find themselves in a particular place of unity. Their lives can be broken or incoherent, but in that place they share an ideal of life and, therefore, their lives are rebuilt. A place of unity has been born throughout the educational process, and this living place is the community. In a school, this is called the school community. The physical place was there before, but the non-physical place was born, manifested itself, in the process.

Chapter 5

A Different Type of School

Vision

What kind of education does the human being need? What kind of school does the human being need in this crucial moment in history? Certainly, not every kind of school can be an adequate answer to these questions. We need a school that wants students to understand the world and themselves. A school that follows the method of integral and human experience, as described in the fourth chapter, is different from the average school. It has a different vision. The vision coincides with the proposal offered to the students, and this vision is clearly expressed through certain signs.

The most visible sign of this school is unity. There is unity because there is one vision, not two or twenty. There is one proposal made to the students. There is one viewpoint of reality as a whole. What builds unity and what guides the school is the same energy that changes our self-awareness and makes it grow.

First, unity exists in the form of friendship among the adults who lead the school: the principal, teachers, and staff. They embody the vision and live it with the rest of the stakeholders, particularly the students. This kind of school is different because the people who work in it are different. Some people act as points of reference that enhance unity: the principal, who serves as a point of reference for the whole school, school leaders, and teacher leaders. In elementary school, every teacher serves as a reference for the students in his classroom. In middle school and high school, the homeroom teacher and the counselor can exercise this reference.

The principal is not a "Lone Ranger" who masters some managerial and pedagogical skills. He masters those skills but he also sets the tone and personifies the vision. Furthermore, he favors the unity and growth of the school community. His living experience in search for meaning engages teachers, students, and families on a journey of knowledge and personal growth. The school community builds itself in this process as a community of learners working and living together. There are fewer conflicts in such a school, because every individual is involved in a communal learning adventure.

Second, there is unity in the form of trust in the relationship between teachers and students. More trust can be built if the same teacher instructs the same student for more than one year. The same can also be said if the same student has the same counselor and homeroom teacher throughout middle school or high school. This is the way a friendship is fostered with the students and their parents. Third, there is unity among counselors, teachers, and parents, expressed through a collaborative relationship in which they know each other, share similar desires, and work together for the good of the students.

Fourth, the teachers encourage unity among students and guide their companionship. U.S. middle schools and high schools typically have a large number of enrolled students. Very often, students do not feel at home and do not have the opportunity to share time and classes with the same peers, making it more difficult to form friendships and complete group work. Many students can feel lost or intimidated in a huge and impersonal school. A way to overcome this difficulty and foster a family environment for the youth is by providing programs in which small groups of students – between 20 and 30 – take a core group of courses together every year throughout the three years of middle school or the four years of high school. Students taking courses with the same classmates develop long-term and meaningful friendships by helping one another through group work and by connecting the knowledge acquired in their real-life experiences. This is how they acquire an integral education and develop the long-term retention of meaningful learning. Students who are unhappy may be switched to other classrooms and replaced by new students. This way the school can meet all the students' needs. Fifth, programs like the aforementioned one can favor unity among families. Parents and siblings of the students who take courses together could meet each other and collaborate with the vision of the school.

In this type of school environment in which the integral experience method is followed, students are educated not by an impersonal institution but by the human experience that they encounter and live in the school. This is relevant to their life's needs. Through human relations, the student tests a hypothesis of meaning, which is proposed by teachers and peers through all subject matters and other elements of the school life such as after-school activities, field trips, and events. The proposal is unified. There is no book discussed, no video watched, no exercise done, and no activity proposed that does not embody an aspect of the proposal. This experience engages them and attracts their interest, because it is relevant to their human needs. The knowledge acquired through the different disciplines and aspects of the environment allows the student to gradually discover the meaning of the larger picture of reality as a whole. Unless the student is immersed in an experience that provides meaning and an answer to the truth of his human-ity, to his life's needs and questions he will not be able to understand a world that proposes the opposite; a world where everything is relative, nothing lasts, and existence has no meaning.

Other schools have other visions and offer different types of proposals. Very often they consider only the utili-tarian needs of the students, ignoring their human needs. In some cases, their administrators would like to change that vision. However, "culture is likely to be harder to change in schools than in other organizations, since schools are by their very nature less entrepreneurial and more bureau-cratic, and since most are mature rather than new institutions."[170] Is it possible to transform the school vi-sion? It is possible if in that school there is a person who is different. With this, I mean a person who embodies a more fulfilling proposal. Without such a presence in that school it would be impossible, because only a meaningful life expe-rience can engage students in a true journey of knowledge.

The integral experience method not only offers a proposal with a different content, but it also offers the proposal in a different way, with a different style. Some schools try to impose a specific school culture without giving students the opportunity to verify it. Thus, the school culture becomes a kind of ideology. The proposal must be offered in a way that makes the student's reason and freedom grow. The student freely verifies the contents of the disciplines and the modalities of the teaching and learning processes. It is important that teachers and students collectively understand the reasons for every single thing that is proposed. The teacher is an authority not because he is a good entertainer or because he exercises power but rather because he verifies the proposal with the student; he makes the student enjoy the discovery of meaning and shows him the hows and whys. The owner of a repair shop does the same thing when his little son is learning the job with him. The goal is not to impose rules or transmit information but rather to live an experience in which the teacher, without ceasing his exploration of reality, encourages the student to work with him, like an apprenticeship.[171] For Segiovanni, "In a learning community, knowledge exists as something that is both individually owned and community owned at the same time. The two feed off each other."[172]

Another component of this integral experience method is the importance of peer learning. Because each student is unique and needs a different amount of time in the verification process, various answers to the hypothesis of meaning are proposed. When students understand the reasons for what is proposed and see the relevance to their life's needs, they embody the school vision too. These students can help their classmates grow in knowledge, freedom, and responsibility. Peer learning is needed when students help each other to understand a concept in class or when group work is developed. However, peer learning is crucial when the interest shared is not a small concept or a class project but rather pertains to higher needs such as friendship, family relations, use of free time, and love. Students can introduce their peers to the universality of the cultural proposal offered by the school and can help them move their uncertain freedom in the right direction.

In this method it is important that not only students but also teachers grow in self-awareness. They do so when they avoid three negative aspects of school life. The first is the transmission of abstract knowledge that is disconnected from particular realities, especially the concrete life of teacher and student. All theories, ideas, or concepts must be rooted in experience. What strikes students is not a discourse but rather a person's presence and experience. The goal is to involve students in a human experience. The second is the academic individualism in which teachers and students do not share knowledge and life with their peers but rather compete with them. Instead of competition, we should cultivate a passion for reality, truth, and the common good. Third is the loss of the sense of teaching and learning as a personal vocation, as a way to grow in humanity and fulfillment.

Finally, although any school – public, charter, private, or religious – can have the vision described above, this school is different especially because it cannot be replicated by following some schemes like clones. Surely such schools would have similarities, but in a certain sense, they are unique because they consist of people with unique personalities, creativity, and responsibility. What they have in common is that these people are certain about a hypothesis of meaning. Because of that, they are able to detect and embrace the truth that can be found in everything and everybody, and therefore they can build a school that is enriched with different traits and creativity but with the same vision. When a model is replicated, only people who fit in can be part of that school. Conversely, a school in which the integral experience method is followed is different because every person –of any cultural background or ethnicity – is embraced and feels at home.

The supreme law of this school environment is charity. The first charity is being loved, being chosen for a task. Teachers are aware of this love and are aware of their need to give themselves. They go to their classrooms every day to satisfy that need. Charity is what moves teachers and sets their ideals and their passion for teaching on fire. When teachers are moved by charity, many of their coworkers and students are moved by charity as well. For this reason, we can define this type of school as a fountain of charity.

Academic Journey

This type of school offers a balanced curriculum with essential subject matters, fundamental contents, and clear objectives instead of a load of information and activities under the form of a supermarket of multiple – and sometimes awkward – options. Globalization, new technologies, and the media flood today's schools and students with massive information and seductive images, but not everything is important or good, and not everything can be learned at the same time and in the same way. The academic journey has to facilitate a systematic method of discernment between what is essential and what is secondary to present a clear picture of how the world works. It should not present disconnected pieces of a torn caricature of the world. In this sense, it is better that the student not be exposed to too many things; he should be exposed only to essential things that he can synthesize with his own reason and retain in the form of meaningful knowledge.

The academic journey has two dimensions: synchronic and diachronic. The first one relates to knowledge as a whole, disciplines, and instruments that the student receives at a certain moment in time. All subject matters have the same dignity but not the same importance; no teacher can distort the curriculum by assigning to his discipline a higher value or by imposing a higher commitment; and all teachers have to collaborate with one another to facilitate the student's work, reinforce each other's subject matters, and help the student make interdisciplinary connections and links with the whole. In this sense, every course is a language course, every teacher teaches the history of his subject matter, and in every discipline, connections with other subject matters are discovered. The diachronic dimension refers to the continuity of the academic journey in time: elementary school, middle school, and high school. Here it is very important to know which units have been covered to avoid unnecessarily repeating notions while being flexible in reinforcing basic and important concepts as needed.[173]

Subject matters must be places where students engage aspects of reality and discover meanings and links with the universal reality. For Nobel Prize laureate Eccles,

"The whole cosmos is not just running on and running down with no meaning."[174] The challenge is to discover those meanings and connections. To this end, it is important to start in all subjects and levels with simple and concrete realities, evolving to abstract and complex concepts. In this direction, effective tools that Novak and Gowin use to design instructional programs and lesson plans are concept mapping and Vee diagramming. These tools allow the student to discover knowledge through meaningful connections.[175] The student has to use his creativity, his imagination, and his power of abstraction, but at the same time, he has to see and experience. A good representation of this journey is a puzzle. The discovery of any little truth is like the discovery of the position of a little piece of the puzzle, because it allows the student to intuit a little part of the whole. Every piece of knowledge illumines other pieces and little by little, the whole manifests itself.

The academic journey requires an interdisciplinary approach to organize knowledge and present its unity. Every subject matter tends to be autonomous by establishing its own boundaries, developing particular concepts and methods, and creating its own specialized language.[176] The academic planning has to respect the integrity of every subject matter and at the same time enrich each by putting all of them in a global perspective that holds them together and signifies more than the addition of each one individually. Thus, new connections and understandings emerge and offer a more unified and meaningful picture of reality. Without these connections it is impossible for students to assimilate and integrate what they receive during six or seven hours of class every day.

The interdisciplinary approach is not to study an object – such as the neighborhood – from different disciplines: economics, language, sociology, history, or art. Rather, it is to reflect on what holds together the different disciplines, the coherence of our culture, and the unity of knowledge.[177] This is the way every concept taught can be compared with a hypothesis of meaning and can be referred to a coherent academic journey, to a student's life experience, and to a unified school vision. A true example of interdisciplinary knowledge and culture can be seen every year at the Meeting of Rimini,[178] one of the world's most attended cultural festivals. Scientists, scholars, educators, politicians, businessmen, artists, and athletes dialogue and show how knowledge and culture express themselves as a fascinating experience.

Important parts of the academic planning are the human, existential, and historical dimensions. If we disregard the meaning of existence, there is no real connection between the past and the present through a human experience and a history, because it allows for only abstract and timeless currents of ideas and structures. The student has to be exposed to the great events and protagonists of history. He must be able to place them in their proper time and dialogue with them. Thus, questions regarding meaning arise in the student, and he is able to link the particular with the universal.

The academic journey pays particular attention to the learning of languages. Language is learned through all subject matters. The student has to be able to express what he has learned in proper writing and speaking; therefore it is important to learn the vocabulary of every subject matter and to be able to distinguish it from colloquial language. A thorough knowledge of language helps the student to develop critical thinking, synthesize information, and grow in self-awareness. Without it, the student cannot demonstrate his knowledge and lived experience.

In this school, sports, field trips, events, and extracurricular activities cannot be devalued to entertainment or to social and instinctive proposals. Very often, these activities acquire tremendous importance, do not achieve important educational goals, and are a burden or weaken the academic journey. Extracurricular activities cannot be the first priority and must be aligned with the academic journey and the school vision. These activities should be encouraged if students find in them a real place of education and a motivation that leads them to be more engaged with the proposed experience and the academic path. These activities should be places where the message implicit in the school vision is clearly communicated. The unity and beauty of school events should be an example of it.

Field days and field trips are important when, inside an ordered setting, students and teachers share passion for knowledge, truth, and life in an atmosphere that fosters unity. On these occasions, teachers and students get to know each other, share life, discover common interests, and witness their human and academic experiences. These days are different from the travel agency's packages. They should be expressions of a fullness of life that can be achieved through the beauty of a place, concert, or museum; through the witness of an important author or public figure; through the visit of a historic place, which reveals our tradition; through the goodness found in a charitable work; or through the wonder awakened by an experiment. During these days, teachers and students explore together, discovering life and the world.

A good academic journey is fundamental for successful learning and includes general and specific goals for each grade level, contents of each course, methodologies to follow, standards and competencies, activities, timing and monitoring of the assimilation of notions, evaluation, extracurricular activities, and required resources. Teacher planning can be flexible to address students' needs, but it must be aligned with the school academic planning and vision. Among the general goals of the academic journey are the following:

- Foster students' curiosity and wonder through the observation of reality.

- Promote critical thinking and a broad concept of reason that uses various procedures to discover knowledge.

- Encourage inquiry and awaken questions for meaning in students, particularly existential questions and questions about the meaning of the different subject matters: What is mathematics? Does history have a meaning?

- Encourage the search for truth and love for truth.

- Favor the experience of the mystery and the experience of reality as signs in which the particular leads to the universal.

- Favor the awareness that every discipline is a channel to access reality and that its educational value depends on its capacity to link its content to reality as a whole.

- Facilitate discovery and promote the experience of knowledge as an event, not only in math and science, but also in all subject matters and other aspects of reality.

- Discourage preconceptions, prejudices, and relativism.

- Clarify and educate the humanity of the student.

- Engage students in a life experience through living an experience in which they test a working hypothesis of the meaning of reality.

- Support the acquisition of certainties, particularly existential certainties.

- Facilitate the links between the student's world and reality so that the student finds new knowledge as part of his experience and relevant to his life's needs and, thus, is engaged in learning.

- Favor a worldview in which the positivity of reality is highlighted.

- Foster peer learning and group work as a way to facilitate personal and social growth.

- Build mutual trust with peers, teachers, and parents.

- Support the use of freedom as a way to grow in maturity and responsibility.

- Stimulate the ability to conduct self-evaluations.

- Involve the student in school life to favor his exposure to the school vision and his participation in the school unity and community.

- Encourage students to embrace diversity and seek unity with others by supporting the certainty of their identity while encouraging them to search for the truth and the good that lives in everybody.

- Provide a synchronic, diachronic, and interdisciplinary view of all subject matters to favor the integration of knowledge and connections with global reality.

- Develop the human dimension through all subject matters by pointing out the existential relevance of their contents, encouraging the study of humanities, history, arts, and including the teaching of history in all areas, particularly in science.

- Stimulate the acquisition of a logical and autonomous method of reasoning and a systematic method of study and assimilation of knowledge.

- Support fascination, search for beauty, and develop creativity and sensitivity for literature and the arts.

- Encourage the knowledge of history to favor the understanding of tradition.

- Foster the mastery of oral and written language as a way to grow in self-awareness, critical thinking, and the understanding of reality.

- Favor the study of vocabulary, and encourage the distinction between technical language and colloquial language.

- Encourage the study of world languages and cultures to grow in understanding of the world.

- Develop a proper integration of technology in teaching and learning to enhance instruction, draw student interest, classify and filter information, and facilitate the integration of knowledge.

- Propose sports, field days, field trips, and extracurricular activities not as entertainment but as places of education connected with the academic journey and the school vision.

Teaching

In the second chapter, it was said that teaching cannot be reduced to training a student to be admitted to a good college or to get a good job. It cannot be the transmission of large amounts of information that the student is unable to interconnect. In addition, education cannot be conceived as indoctrination, sometimes disguised as fake neutrality, because the student has freedom and reason. In the same way, education cannot be reduced to the teaching of some values and behaviors, because the student cannot be reduced to psychology and sociology. Finally, teaching cannot be reduced to entertainment. For Steiner, "Bad teaching is... a sin. It diminishes the student; it reduces to gray inanity the subject being presented. It drips into the child's or the adult's sensibility that most corrosive of acids, boredom, the marsh gas of ennui."[179]

Obviously, teachers need to master their subject matters. They have to be able to communicate them and must be able to work under the spotlight every day, managing their emotions and the emotions of their students. We could enumerate many characteristics of what everybody commonly understands as good teaching. However, what kind of teaching is needed to educate the whole human being? What kind of teaching is needed to provide him with the maps that he needs to properly understand himself and to understand reality? This kind of teaching is different; it is more than following certain procedures and achieving certain goals. It is true child-centered education, because it is focused on the student and is the cultivation of the human. Let us see some traces of it.

The first one is certainty. A teacher who is certain of who he is and what it means to teach can use his life experiences to challenge the freedom and reason of his students. He can propose his worldview to them and invite them to verify it. Only someone who understands himself can help others to understand themselves. This certainty has to be an important ideal, something that gives life and deserves the dedication of our whole lives. In the presence of a teacher with such certainty, students are not foolish and decide to build their foundations on that rock, on the teacher's certitude. This teacher has the right to demand attention and preparation from his students because his passion for communicating what he knows and what he lives makes him creative, patient, and able to make big sacrifices for the sake of building human beings.

The second one is that he makes the student's humanity and certainty grow through the teaching of his subject matter. The student grows because the teacher does not unload what he knows on him; rather, he invites the student to grow with him in his personal relationship with his subject matter and with reality. This requires that the teacher have a sense of the unity and universality of knowledge and that he be able to develop interdisciplinary syntheses. There are teachers who master very particular specialties extraordinarily well, but who have little understanding of reality as a whole.

The teacher works at the service of the student's discovery. The student matures by exploring the road of reality opened by the discipline and accompanied by the teacher. The student sees reality through the eyes of the teacher and the great protagonists of history, authors, or scientists; he does this by testing their hypotheses, walking in their shoes, connecting his personal life with their personal lives, asking himself their questions, reformulating them, and searching for answers. This method of teaching and learning does not imprison the student in small and abstract concepts that he finds useless, but enables him to open such concepts to the universality of the great problems and questions of the world. Thus, the class is more than fun without the need of multimedia or entertainment fireworks. It is fulfilling because, through concrete and small contents of a subject matter, the student discovers meaningful things, even mysteries of mankind.

This teacher, through the way he teaches mathematics – or language or history – is able to bring out the best in the student: autonomous critical thinking; the capacity to synthesize mathematical truths and connect them with the rest of the disciplines and with the student's life experience and needs; freedom from peer pressure and freedom to become responsible for his own learning; creativity and curiosity; self-esteem and sense of great personal value, even when academic achievement is still low or when personal problems suffocate him; docility when he is corrected; generosity in his relationship with peers; and solid knowledge and convictions.

The third trace of this different style of teaching is true affection between teacher and student. This has an impact in terms of student behavior. Marzano says, "If a teacher has a good relationship with students, then students more readily accept the rules and procedures and the disciplinary actions that follow their violations."[180] However, teachers are neither students' friends nor their accomplices. Rather, the teacher becomes the generator of the student's humanity, and therefore, he becomes a kind of second father for the student. The teacher becomes an authority for the student, not because of his role, but because he gives his life for the student. This generates a reciprocal affection of the student for his teacher, which is visible in terms of respect and admiration. Furthermore, when a student is "affected" by his teacher, he is also affected by his subject matter. This dynamic logically entails an improvement in student academic achievement. For these reasons it is best to avoid substituting the physical relationship of teacher-student for other pedagogical methods such as distance learning.

Another characteristic is that in this different type of school, nobody teaches alone. However, this is not the reality in our country. For Donaldson, "American public schools were not designed to be led in the ways that we now exhort leaders to attempt."[181] He holds that "teachers in many schools operate like planets in a galactic subsystem, maintaining their own orbit and unique classrooms spin."[182] These teachers may have talents and passion for their jobs, but their lessons do not build unity in a school. Their students will be affected by problems similar to the ones that affect families with divorced parents.[183] Unity in a school reminds us of a family in which there is love. To teach is a communitarian dynamic. What really educates is a community, through its history and culture.

Not teaching alone implies that there is a community of teachers as well as one school vision that is shared by them. To this end, it is particularly important that teachers understand that they share common goals and are responsible not only for their subject matters but also for an educational journey that demands a communitarian commitment.[184] There is a dialogue in which the English teacher becomes interested in the ancient Greek civilization –taught by the history teacher – and helps his students to connect what they learn in history with the Pythagorean theorem taught in the mathematics class. Meanwhile the history and math teachers correct the language of the English literature students and even show interest in the poem that these students have to analyze in their homework. These types of teachers become friends, share ideas, correct one another, and enjoy what they do.

This style of teaching also fosters academic achievement. Louis and Marks, in a study of 24 successful schools, discovered that the most successful showed higher levels of student achievement because teachers had a shared mission and a firm sense of community.[185]

Another indicator is that in this school, teaching is considered a calling. "Authentic teaching is a vocation," says Steiner. "The teacher is aware of the magnitude and, if you will, mystery of his profession... he has taken vows."[186] A teacher who is aware of the mystery of his profession and of his life can help his students become aware of the mystery of their lives and of the mystery hidden in their books. However, the truth of this vocation is tested in the small details of daily life, in the way we are attentive to the needs of our students and our coworkers, in the way we sow the seeds of our humanity. We are not in our schools by chance or wandering like nomads from one place to another. We have seriously considered following our call by planting our roots in that place. Our call is a call to communicate an experience to our students and to our coworkers that matches their human needs. This is why teachers go to school every day; it is not a sentiment but rather a fullness of life. Teachers communicate the humanity that overflows from them, and when they do so, the humanity of the people around them, through osmosis, thrives.

Finally I would like to refer to the way professional development is different in this school. For teachers – not only for students – schools are learning and inquiring communities.[187] Teachers learn from other teachers, for example, when they visit their classrooms and observe them. However, this has been an unusual practice in many schools. Teachers almost never see their colleagues perform, particularly in high school. Teachers in the same department can learn from each other by planning together and sharing talents, experiences, and choices. They can learn together how to develop a cultural revision of the curriculum: identifying which contents, readings, or activities are essential for the growth of the students' humanity.

The worst teacher is the one who thinks that he knows it all, because each must continually grow. However, what kind of growth are we talking about? This growth is that which is learned through the integral experience that we live. This experience enables us to personalize and enhance the competencies and knowledge that we have acquired in the past and continue to acquire in the present. We can generate our students if we live an experience of teaching that is generating our inner being. This is what gives us an extraordinary intelligence of reality, challenges our students, and makes us gain their respect: the fact that they see us incessantly being generated.

Learning

This school shows that it is child-centered because, among other factors, teaching depends on learning and is focused on the student. In this school, learning is a search and love for truth that fosters the growth of the student's freedom and responsibility.

Learning is not only a cognitive process; it is also a human process because it involves the whole of the human being, with his reason, freedom, and longings. Without the implication of all the dimensions of the person, the student is not truly involved; he does not take the initiative; and if he learns something, that learning is not accompanied by fulfillment. The mere transmission of information to the student is not meaningful learning, because he has to use his reason to test new knowledge and assimilate it. The student tests new knowledge by comparing it with his longing for truth, which causes him to continue the process until he is able to connect the particular with the universal. Once he has verified this piece of new knowledge, he has to relate it to prior knowledge and see that it is coherent with it. This type of learning requires the implication of the best of the student – his intellect, his affection, and his desire for truth

– but it is highly rewarding because it provides more than wisdom; it provides human fulfillment.

In the fourth chapter, it was said that the educative dialogue requires the involvement of both the teacher's and the student's freedom. Both parties collaborate in a common goal; it is like a contract: "I will speak, if you will listen. I will come here to learn, if you have any thing worth teaching me."[188] Locke would say: "The sooner you treat him as a man, the sooner he will begin to be one."[189] What is key is to respect the mystery of the student's being and to bet on his freedom so that he can take the initiative to enter into a relationship with that mystery and discover it. Camus, in his unfinished novel *The First Man* published by his daughter 35 years after his death in 1960, shows his human experience with his teacher – using both the figurative name and the real name:

> "No, school did not just provide them an escape from family life. At least in M. Bernard's class, it fed a hunger in them more basic even to the child than to the man, and that is the hunger for discovery. No doubt they were taught many things in their other classes, but it was somewhat the way geese are stuffed: food was presented to them and they were asked to please swallow it. In M. Germain's class, they felt for the first time that they existed and that they were the objects of the highest regard: they were judged worthy to discover the world."[190]

The student has many desires. He experiences freedom when his desires are satisfied. In the *Divine Comedy*, Dante says that "each one confusedly a good conceives wherein the mind may rest, and longeth for it; therefore to overtake it each one strives."[191] One of these desires is the longing for truth. In fact, the attainment of truth makes us free. Every meaning that the student discovers causes him to experience satisfaction. However, his heart cannot find rest until he is completely satisfied, fulfilled. Therefore, what is crucial is to educate his freedom so that he can enlarge his desires and grow in fulfillment. His freedom is aided through companionship. The student does not learn alone, but in a learning community. His parents, his teachers, and his peers accompany his freedom and make it grow.

However, although the student does not learn alone, it has to be his decision and his responsibility. A positive sign of growth in responsibility for his own learning is that the student chooses what to study and how to do it. A student shows his engagement in learning when, for example, he is looking for the materials that he needs, he is preparing the lesson, or he is organizing his time. Teachers can nurture this positive attitude in their students, especially if they see why things are proposed in a certain way. Students develop self-discipline and responsibility when they are involved in classroom management and when they are part of the decision-making process.

Going to school is an experience of freedom and fulfillment for the student when he identifies with the teachers and when his learning trusts and follows the invitations, reasons, and corrections of their teaching. A student with this attitude can have the joy of discovering meaningful learning with subject matters or with teachers that he does not like or who are less talented. Even in these circumstances, it is truly rewarding to see mysteries being un-

veiled before our eyes. "We have seen that Mastery is fallible," says Steiner, but if we really love truth, then nothing
can eliminate "the daybreak we experience when we have
understood a Master. That joy does nothing to alleviate
death. But it makes one rage at its waste. Is there no time
for another lesson?"[192]

Now I will refer to four aspects of learning in which
the uniqueness of this type of school can be observed. The
first one deals with student motivation and the way students' curiosity and interest is awakened. The second one is
critical thinking. The third one refers to the concept of
studying and the way the youth studies in this school. The
fourth is the integration of technology in learning.

Attracting Students' Interest

There are many reasons students may not be interested in
learning or do not participate in class. The most common is
that learning, in their opinion, has nothing to do with them,
what they love, and what they need. Therefore, their freedom is not engaged. The attraction of the interest depends
on two elements. The first one is the love that the student
has for himself and for his fulfillment. The second one is
the communicative and osmotic force with which concepts
in class are presented and make the student perceive their
meaning.[193] Aristotle would say, "Things that are true and
things that are just have a natural tendency to prevail over
their opposites."[194] Aquinas would answer, "Bonum est dif-
fusivum sui" (Good pours itself out).[195] Truth has a natural
tendency to attract, and goodness spreads itself out. Therefore, awakening student interests, above all, is a matter of
letting truth, justice, goodness, and beauty flow in our les-

sons and classrooms and letting them reach our students' longings (for truth, justice, goodness, and beauty).

The impact on the heart of the student is the fire that ignites it. This is what awakens his interest in everything.[196] More important than external incentives is the need to target the personal experience and the inner self of the student in all its dimensions. Thus, the student is intrinsically motivated, struck, and captivated, and his whole self is involved: his affection, his intellect, and his body (the student moves, works, asks, collaborates). His freedom is moved by his desire to enter into a relationship with the world and to know it. Interest in something does not come from will power but from the impact with reality. When any reality moves the student, the student is glued to it. When the student understands something, that adhesion is even more empowered.

To this end, it is important that the teacher embrace all of his students with his gaze, show interest for the object studied, and share his personal interests with them, such as why he studied mathematics and all its equations and why he became a teacher. In the words of Camus: "With M. Bernard, this class was always interesting for the simple reason that he loved his work with a passion... only the flies during a storm could sometimes divert the children's attention... but M. Bernard's... would win out over even the flies."[197]

When the student is drawn by the teacher's interest, he generates a reciprocal dynamic on the teacher. Students always have something to offer; they are not empty bottles to be filled. Teachers always learn from them and with them. It is crucial for teacher and student to observe reality together, to interpret its signs, and to be involved in the truth that happens before their eyes. There is nothing more attractive than truth. In this manner, teacher and student share the interest for exploring together, for discovering reality together.

Many people believe that student interest and curiosity are only a matter of pedagogical methods and techniques. People highlight the importance of integrating technology in learning, changing the tone of voice, or changing frequently the class dynamic. I do not want to disregard the importance of these issues, but I want to highlight the relevance of letting the student be struck by the impact of reality: "If I were to open my eyes for the first time in this instant, emerging from my mother's womb," – says Giussani – "I would be overpowered by the wonder and awe of things as a presence."[198]

If teacher and student are in class with this awareness, everything shocks their consciousness and stimulates their intellect and curiosity. The manifestation of reality affects us not because it stimulates our senses in a mechanical way, but because it concerns us and carries signs of meaning. Rubbia, Nobel Prize laureate in physics, says that "When we look at a particular physical phenomenon, for example a starry night, we feel deeply moved; we feel within ourselves a message which comes from nature, which transcends it and dominates it."[199] In fact, the etymology of desire is "lack of stars". The word "desire" comes from the Latin "de" which means "lack" and "sidus –eris," which means "a group of stars". If we look at the stars with our students, they speak to us, and we are so moved that all of us desire them. Newman describes very well the dynamic of curiosity and the experience of the search for truth: "We desire to see, to hear, and to learn; and consider the knowledge of what is hidden or is wonderful a condition of our happiness."[200]

Beauty is one of the most powerful signs of meaning and has the capacity to awaken every single human being. In Leopardi's poem *On the Portrait of a Beautiful Lady* we see how beauty creates longings for the infinite: "If, human nature, then, in all things fallible, you are but dust and shade, whence these high feelings?"[201] This poem shows why beauty both wounds our humanity and is the splendor of truth. Music is another exceptional way to perceive beauty as the splendor of truth. Through the beauty of music, the mystery speaks to man's heart.

For this reason, it is amazing to see how a chemist is fascinated by an experiment, how a mathematician finds beauty in the midst of many formulas, or how a physicist is fascinated by the regularities of tiny particles. For the Nobel Prize laureate in medicine Konrad Lorenz, "Every human being who can become sentient to and experience joy in creation and its beauty is made immune to any and every doubt about its meaning."[202] Schools should be places where teachers and students are wounded by beauty and its meaning.

Finally, I would like to highlight the importance of questions. We learn things because we pose questions. Sometimes questions are out of place, conceited, disrupting, or confused, but they can be part of the cement of learning. Questions that relate to what we are doing, what is expected, why we do it, and what this is about show that the student is engaged, interested, and aware of the lesson's goals. The test that shows whether a lesson really engaged the students is if they continued the discussion when the class was over.[203]

However, teachers cannot be happy in satisfying only some of their students' basic intellectual needs or curiosities. Students and teachers have the same thirst for the infinite and are challenged by the same dilemmas of life. By addressing the basic needs or questions of the students, the teacher can awaken their existential questions and their thirst for meaning. This is what really involves students in learning and engages them with their real lives. When students are engaged in reality, genuine questions arise, and solid meanings are grasped.

Critical Thinking

This section makes reference to what was discussed with regard to verifying the hypothesis and the use of reason in the fourth chapter.

Most experts agree on the importance of critical thinking. The problem is that many teaching styles contradict this concept. More and more education is identified with the transmission of information and less and less with the growth of students' freedom and reason. John Locke says that reasoning with a child and seeing him reflect upon what is proposed, "Gives him a liking to study and instruction."[204] It is key that teaching follows the same path of reasoning that learning should follow so that students grow and become self-teachers and independent reasoners.[205] This is possible when teachers and students reason together and discover meanings together.

Metalearning and metaknowledge are very important: to help students learn about learning and to help
them understand the structure of knowledge and the
journey followed in its acquisition. Students should be
able to connect new concepts with their previous knowledge by building road maps that show relationships between ideas, breaking through textbooks and other readings, and discovering implications from projects and
laboratories.[206]

There are different ways to develop critical thinking
in our lessons: to explain, to demonstrate, and to argue. To
explain means to show the position of a particular thing in
the whole. The relevance of that concrete thing depends on
its capacity to lead to a more universal knowledge of reality. To demonstrate, particularly important in science, is to
display the truth of a statement from the truth – already
evident – of another. However, a demonstration is not always possible. That is why it is important to argue – in the
sense of being reasonable – not for pursuing knowledge but
in a pragmatic way in our daily life.[207]

We could mention three more ways to foster critical
thinking in our students. The first one is to make students
reason about what interests them to engage their attention
during the whole path of reasoning proposed. The second
one is to foster self-esteem for the student's reason. The
third one is to encourage respect among students, so that
contention is not developed among them during class discussions, but rather a friendly collaboration in which they
learn from the viewpoints of one another and from the dif-

ferent ways that they use their reasons.[208]

Students are often not engaged in learning because they do not know how to read reality, how to grasp meanings. They are unable to do it because they did not develop their critical thinking. Pedagogical methods and technology certainly can help, but this issue is primarily a matter of discovering meanings through critical thinking. However, not only children, but also adults, have mistakenly interpreted the goal of reason. Frequently it is not a path to truth, but a weapon that we use to convince others or to defend ourselves when others try to convince us.[209] This is the kind of reason that we see in many reality shows and debates between politicians on television.

How can our reason grasp how the world works? How can we read reality? For the father of quantum physics, Max Planck, "The laws of human reasoning coincide with the laws governing the sequences of the impressions we receive from the world about us; therefore, pure reasoning can enable man to gain an insight into the mechanism of the latter."[210]

In Spanish, to teach is "enseñar", which comes from the Latin "insignio –ire" (to mark, to distinguish) and "signo –are" (to mark, to indicate). It is the teacher's responsibility to point to the signs that he sees, to share signs, helping the student to read reality. When a student says that he does not like mathematics, it usually is because he does not know how "to read it". A student discovers a mathematical truth when he sees concrete numbers and concepts blending together and becoming a more universal reality.

The problem is that teaching and learning often devalue the use of reason. It does so in two ways. One is through facilitating the understanding so much that there is a total simplification and almost no critical thinking. Teachers provide information but do not stimulate reasoning or awaken questions of meaning in their students. Instead, critical thinking should be about encouraging students to walk with their teachers on a journey through the discovery of senses. Secondly, it denies the students the possibility of arguing about existential questions and final causes. Students are bored when subject matters are not what they should be: open roads to the knowledge of life and reality. Such a method does not encourage the use of an agile and broad reason engaged in multiple paths to explain reality in all its factors and all students' human experiences. Only an open use of reason corresponds to the students' longing for truth.

Studying

This is one of the biggest problems that students face. Many of them solve it by escaping from it; they do not study. Others study only when they are forced to do so. The rest study, but only because they have to. For all of them, it is a big sacrifice, and they long for graduation day, the moment in which their real lives will start. Extrinsic motivations – ranging from moral appeals, to gifts, to longings for success – usually do not work, because even if they make the individual study, the student sees no sense in that sacrifice and remains unsatisfied.

To help them, parents and teachers suggest many strategies and techniques: ways to be more focused, the development of certain habits, correction of external conditions such as noise and light, and many more. Sometimes parents overreact to their children's learning problems and constantly seek the help of psychologists, tutors, and other specialists when, in reality, there is no need to do so. I acknowledge the importance of many of those pedagogical strategies, and I believe specialists are a great help when students have real need of them. However, a different approach to the concept of studying may solve these issues.

The term "study" comes from the Latin word "studium," which means zeal, eagerness, enthusiasm, striving, application to learning. "Studiosus," in Latin, is a person devoted to learning, a person with a fervent eagerness to know. The etymology of the word "study" clearly underlines its nature: attraction, love, and eagerness. For Aquinas, it is "vehemens applicatio mentis," a vigorous application of the mind.[211] Dante conceives it as an "application of the soul in love."[212] For Augustine, "Nourishes the mind only what pleases it."[213]

Therefore, the way to deal with the sacrifice of studying is to connect it with the joy of satisfying our deepest need for truth and fulfillment. Thus, studying becomes the loving search for the truth of things, and satisfaction is found in the application to the discovery of a concept, because it is conceived as the attainment of a piece of truth and as a step in the personal journey toward fulfillment. A student might consider a concrete aspect of a subject matter interesting, but its real interest lies in its link with his human fulfillment, which is what actually satisfies.

For example, when a student has a particular aversion to math or history, the question that he has to ask himself is how mathematics or history relates to him, his interests, and his fulfillment. It is important to help him see this link, maybe through another subject that he likes. If he does see the link – through this or another subject –, he achieves something more valuable than a good grade on a test, because through that link he satisfies his hunger for meaning and begins to experience passion for discovering other aspects of reality. This is owned and real critical thinking applied to studying, which is far different from studying by memorization. This experience is also far different from the concept of studying for the future, for a good college, or for a good career. To study for an absent future does not save us from the present hardships, because we want life to be a beautiful adventure today through our courses, textbooks, and notes. Only an experience of true satisfaction in the present can overcome all fatigues.

This experience is lived when reality awakens and attracts us. If an adolescent is in love, he is filled with curiosity and wants to know more about the person loved: what she likes, what she does, and so on. When a student goes back to his desk and finds a closed envelope addressed to him, he is filled with curiosity, and many questions arouse his interest, such as what is inside and who gave it to him. In the same way, when we are open to discovering any reality, many questions assail us, because we want to know what is inside and what it means.

To study also means to dialogue with authors, heroes, or scientists who, although they are dead, suddenly come to life through a book. Literature, history, science, and mathematics are roads built by them. That is why, if we want to learn, we have to study, which entails dialoguing with them, learning why a person made a certain decision, how a scientist had that intuition, and so on.

However, there are live people who can help students develop this dialogue: teachers and classmates. If we want students to navigate the waters of their studies and arrive at the port, they need a captain – the teacher – to guide them. We should not forget that the first and best aid while studying is attentiveness to the teacher and to the lesson. The teacher is not the enemy attempting to defeat the students, but rather is the best ally to prevent them from getting lost and sinking. The teacher offers hypotheses we must transform into certainties through our study, verifying that by pointing the bow of the sailboat in a certain direction, we catch more wind and move faster. Every certainty is a new step on the journey.

It is also important for students to learn from their classmates during the lessons and to study with them after school. Our classrooms and schools are learning communities. According to Sergiovanni, "A particular student's own individual growth and accumulated knowledge contributes to the shared growth and accumulated knowledge that exists in a classroom as a whole. As this accumulated knowledge expands, so does individual knowledge."[214] For example, it is crucial to see the interest and questions that a reading, notion, or problem awakens in other classmates. It is good to study in groups even if students are working on different subject matters. Three people can sit together reading three different books in silence, and this is good. Curiosity, interest, and good habits are communicated through osmosis. However, precisely because group work can be turned into no work, it is a great idea to join people who take it seriously and like studying.

As a great example of what peer learning and group work are, Einstein describes how a friend helped him solve a problem and formulate the theory of specific relativity:

> "Unexpectedly a friend of mine in Bern then helped me. That was a very beautiful day when I visited him and began to talk with him as follows: 'I have recently had a question which was difficult for me to understand. So I came here today to bring with me a battle on the question'. Trying a lot of discussions with him, I could suddenly comprehend the matter. Next day I visited him again and said to him without greeting: Thank you. I've completely solved the problem."[215]

When students study, they need a method and some instruments in addition to companions. Some tools are given to the student: assignments, homework, guidelines, and textbooks; others have to be personally developed, such as order, habit, timing, and procedures. The most important part of the method is to facilitate the assimilation of what they study. The captain of the boat keeps a logbook; students have to do the same. After studying a chapter in the history book, examining the skeleton of an animal, or solving some problems, students have to be able to write something down: what they liked, what they did not understand, what they learned, and, hopefully, its link with their fulfillment as human beings. If they do this, they will gradually improve their study method; they will create a habit; they will be able to attain meaningful learning, and studying will be a gratifying experience.

Technology and Media

In different investigations developed during the '70s and '80s, Kulik and other researchers found that computer-based education improves academic results.[216] However, other investigations concluded the opposite, claiming that computers were only vehicles through which content is delivered and that the real cause of academic improvement was content enhancement.[217]

Today, although there is not enough literature to clearly determine the impact of digital textbooks, electronic tablets, and other technological devices on instruction, it is evident that technology, media, and social networks are transforming school life and education. Schools that do not adopt the "technological revolution" are viewed as boring because they offer abstract knowledge that is disconnected from the interests of students. The education that really shapes students' lives seems to come after school through the media, social networks, and videogames, with their speed and seductive images, that deliver more information and fantasies than students could imagine. In fact, far more information exists outside the classrooms than inside. Amidst this situation, there are parents and teachers who joyfully embrace any technology and the latest media as their new cult, because they believe that education will one day be a matter of "touching the screen." Others are alarmed at the situation and emphasize the serious risks that new technologies, particularly social networks, entail.

What should be the approach to technology and

media in the school environment? First, we have to admit the crucial role that new technologies play in our global world. Second, schools delivering instruction through electronic tablets, interactive eBooks, and smart boards more easily engage students in learning than schools that do not use such devices. Students love using multiple electronic devices. Third, technology and media can greatly enhance instruction if certain guarantees are provided, such as security and filters, an acceptable use policy, adequate classroom management, and the encouragement of critical thinking.

Fourth, a distinction needs to be made that schools are places of education, whereas some media and social network outlets are simply not education in nature. When teachers use new technologies, they have to make sure that they do not substitute the students' search for truth and the use of reason with accumulating information, evocate superficial feelings, or for entertainment. As a rule, no technology, software, app, media, documentary, or film should be used in the classroom unless it clearly enhances instruction. Fifth, new technologies and media can be used to distort the concept of what a human being is, introducing erroneous anthropology into our schools and homes. Parents, teachers, and students are constantly bombarded by ambiguous images and ideas that confuse them; furthermore, they also become agents of a culture that diminishes our humanity by creating ruthless, sentimental, virtual, or lewd realities. The case of U.S. Congressman Anthony D. Weiner might be considered such an example, as he had to resign because of a "sexting" scandal.

Technology is taking over our schools but not technology education. Teachers and administrators confuse technology education with instruction on how to use technology, forgetting that such education also implies teaching to analyze and discern the use of technology and the content that it carries. For this reason, technology education should not be a technical subject but rather a branch of the humanities.[218]

Technology education cannot be confused with strategies implemented to attract students' interest, or to occupy or amuse them. Technology education involves educating with technology to activate in the student the capacity to discern the adequate use of technology and media and to distinguish what is essential from what is secondary, false, only informative, or noneducational. Technology education also entails integrating technology and media with learning in a way that assists instruction without manipulating it, overloading it with excessive or meaningless information, or making it difficult for the student to distinguish fantasy from reality. Furthermore, technology and digital books should not establish a curriculum's content. Administrators and teachers must establish a curriculum's content, standards, benchmarks, and assessments, and then they have to find the adequate technology, eBooks, and other instructional resources to ensure that the instruction is enhanced and aligned with the curriculum to guarantee that students master the benchmarks. To this end, administrators and teachers should customize their own digital books and instructional resources when possible.

Technology education also means not cancelling in the student the practice of memorization and other cognitive exercises that allow him to exercise his reasoning skills, linking the concrete with the abstract and the particular with the universal. In properly addressing these issues, we avoid having the speed of the new technologies transform the students' intellect into bulks of information and sequences of disconnected ideas.

Teachers should not ignore new technologies and media, especially when their students use them after school. They should understand them and help their students to understand them and, when possible, to use their potential. To this end, it is important to distinguish which technologies have educational value and when they should be used. One example is the use of the Internet. Almost every teacher encourages students to conduct research on the Internet but the students' work is often poor academically. This can also happen when videos and other fancy artifacts accompany the students' research. The problem is that we have to teach them how to use it and how to discern its content.

Regarding the use of social media, it is good to value what attracts students to it, such as the desire to make friends, to communicate, and to share notes. However, it is important to be cautious. Social media should be discouraged when it confuses their certainties, when it becomes an addiction or a poor use of free time, when it becomes a place to meet strangers or a place for bullying, or when it isolates students by making them emphasize virtual relations and avoid real face-to-face relationships. Very often, social media ends up building a wall that separates students from reality and creates confusion around them and in their personal relations.

Assessment

What is the true result of a good education? How can one evaluate it? Is it possible to assess the growth of the students' humanity? These questions make us understand that it is not enough to observe the achievement of certain objectives or skills.

In a school that follows the integral experience method, assessment is not an end in itself but rather a part of the learning process. It is focused on "evaluation" – the discovery of value, not mistakes. It encourages the student and it provides praise. It is more than measurement according to certain criteria or standards. It is simultaneously objective and creative, following different procedures. It controls the teaching-learning process, assesses learning, and has an impact on the school structures. It also includes the students' self-evaluation.

Learning and assessment cannot be separated from the student and his personal circumstances. Academic results sometimes reflect the students' ups and downs due to personal problems, a sickness, or a lack of motivation. Sometimes assessment also involves stress and fear. When the student feels loved at home, by his peers, and by his teachers, he tends to perform better academically. The teacher should not stress negative results or mistakes, but he should guide the student by providing feedback, correcting his weak points, and being attentive to acknowledge any progress, and positive value. For this reason, assessment cannot be reduced to assigning letters or numbers to the students; it also must provide student's growth.[219]

Assessment is a moment of learning in which the student's reason and freedom are empowered. Teacher and student see together why specific standards or goals are established, certain evaluation procedures are followed, and concrete results are achieved. When the student is convinced by the reasons, his freedom is motivated. Thus, he synthesizes the knowledge discovered and the knowledge that remains to be discovered; he perceives his weaknesses, his strengths, and his growth; he verifies the educational path proposed by the teacher and the school; and he takes ownership and adheres to it.[220] This is the way assessment engages the student in a relationship with the teacher in a journey of knowledge, and it provides a global vision of a certain path.

Assessment has to be objective, but it is more than measurement. What is needed is to define well what is essential, what is important, what should be taught in every subject, what should be assessed, how it should be assessed – in terms of criteria and procedures –, and what actions should be pursued after the assessment. Not all subjects or learning contents should have the same value. Likewise, even if the course syllabus has a perfect grade breakdown, not all things can be measured. For this reason, assessment has to be creative, following different procedures. According to Ravitch, multiple-choice tests are useful measures of student achievement in a concrete moment, but to enhance the quality of education, assessments should include "research papers in history, essays and stories in literature, research projects in science, demonstrations of mathematical competence, videotaped or recorded conversations in a foreign language, performances in the arts, and other exhibitions of learning."[221]

Assessments in which the student has to express himself, such as essays and oral interviews, require more assessment time and more work for the teacher, but they are particularly important in all subject matters. The student should be able to communicate in writing and speaking what he has learned about the subject matter and about himself. When students do not find words to express their knowledge and experience of reality, they are showing that they have received a poor education. Oral exams are important because they show the general status of a student's knowledge, the way that knowledge is structured, and the way it is evoked. Students' expression is also important when the teacher provides feedback after a test. In this moment, the dialogue with the students and among the students is significant. Teacher and students review the material and learn from one another as new aspects emerge during the discussion.

Assessment controls the teaching-learning process and provides crucial information to improve learning: identifying students in need, better teaching methods, contents to reinforce, and ways that school structures could serve learning better. Standardized testing provides an important and clear point of reference outside of the school. Defining a core of contents and standards and comparing levels of achievement is crucial. However, standardized tests measure fewer things than they omit. That is why test scores cannot be the only way to measure the quality of a school. Ongoing teacher assessment is fundamental to show the path of knowledge and to value, support, and guide students' skills in a way that standardized testing does not measure in issues such as creativity, oral expression, and human growth.

Self-evaluation is another important aspect of assessment. Students usually define themselves through their own self-images and preconceptions. For example, we hear it said that the student's value relates to the school that he attends or the grades that he earns. To avoid preconceptions, the student has to learn to discover himself, to watch himself in action, in his experience, especially in his learning experience. This is how humanity emerges. Self-evaluation is also a way for the student to learn from the teacher's evaluation: the quality of his learning experience, his weaknesses and strengths, his progress, the way he is aware of the testing criteria and procedures, and his position in the journey of knowledge.

Guidance

Guidance is usually understood in terms of orientation. In concrete moments of the academic year, the student meets with a counselor who provides some information to the student and helps him choose from among different courses. During middle school the counselor helps the student join a good high school, and during high school, the counselor helps him to get accepted into a good college. A great deal of the work at the guidance department is spent in trying to help the student obtain better grades so that he will be able to attend a better college. From this perspective, guidance is focused on the student's academic results.

In what way is guidance different in the school that we are discussing in the present chapter? First, we must acknowledge that, as the academic results of the student are important, we cannot disregard his human success, his fulfillment. However, the two types of success are not always found together. The main goal of guidance is to make the human factors of the young person emerge, such as his true identity and his sense of self-awareness. This goal is achieved when the student uses his freedom and reason to pursue his personal growth, his vocation, and his destiny. In this sense it is better not to impose particular choices on the student but rather encourage the student's preferences – in the form of intuitions of truth, beauty, and fruitfulness – to come out. To guide somebody means to continuously help him understand his experience and find his path in life. Counselors and teachers must work together to accompany students in the discovery of their true selves by stimulating their freedom so that they learn to use their reasoning skills and to make their own choices.

The counselor is involved in the life of the student in helping him to understand himself and his reality. The counselor helps the student face his difficulties, listens to his worries and clarifies them, gives him a method of knowledge, awakens his desire to understand and to learn, empowers his talents, helps him optimize his time, creates synergies in the student's journey of growth, and establishes a collaborative relationship between student, teachers, and parents.

In this sense, self-evaluation and guidance are connected. The counselor coordinates the student's interdisciplinary learning and helps him to reflect on his journey of knowledge and its connection with his personal human fulfillment. With this help, the student not only finds the interest to commit to his own studies but also makes sense of his own discoveries of reality, his place in the world, and his destiny.

Discipline

The term discipline comes from the Greek "διδάσκω" and the Latin "disco-discere-didici," which means, "to learn." The Latin term "disciplina" means instruction, teaching, that which is taught, training, and education, but it also refers to discipline and an ordered way of life. Therefore, the etymology of discipline does not emphasize the negative connotations that we usually associate with this word, such as misbehavior, fear, rules, or punishment. Discipline is not an end in itself but rather is a condition and an important element of learning. Discipline facilitates the learning process.

The order and beauty of the universe and of any reality awaken our curiosity to know it and allow us to discover its meaning. For this reason a school needs order and beauty, and the teaching-learning activities need order and beauty. Students are more apt to discover the beauty of their lives and to grasp the meaning of the world when there is order in their lives, particularly in their classrooms. Order has an inner beauty. When students discover it, they become builders of order and builders of beauty.

Plato said "of all animals the boy is the most unmanageable, inasmuch as he has the fountain of reason in him not yet regulated; he is the most insidious, sharp-witted, and unsubordinated of animals."[222] Schools spend many resources and much time dealing with discipline issues. Every school has a dean of discipline, who is usually very busy. Every teacher has confrontations with students and students are sent to the office for various reasons, from the pointless to the serious. It is better not to burden students with many rules, because either we will have to punish constantly or we will have to let many transgressions of the rules go unpunished. Anyway, multiple or harsh punishments very often do more harm than good.

We always have to consider a counseling approach to discipline. Discipline, more than a matter of controlling the behavior of students and limiting their freedom, is a matter of seeing with them the motives behind why things are proposed in a certain way, patiently and inviting their freedom to adhere. Imposing authority and forcing freedom without reasons does not work. As Locke points out, "a child will learn three times as much when he is in tune as he will with double the time and pains when he goes awkwardly or is dragged unwillingly to it."[223] The challenge for the adults is to awaken the students' interest in freely participating in the educational dialogue to the point that they experience inner satisfaction. This satisfaction is what makes them embody the educational proposal and the school vision.

However, the invitation to personalize the school vision cannot be mistaken with exaggerated empathy or relationships based on sentimentality. It is wrong to allow students to do whatever they want, to avoid correcting them, or to spare them the sacrifice of opening the books and doing their homework. The teacher makes the student study and invites him to verify what is taught. The student goes to the class to learn, and he tests the view of reality presented by the teacher through the subject matter. Accountable and responsible teaching does not oppose the regular development of subject matter teaching of the pedagogical relationship of teacher-student;[224]   rather, it blends them in a true and fulfilling educational experience in which both teacher and student grow.

At the same time, it is important not to underestimate the incoherence that accompanies the life of any human being, especially that of the youth in the turbulent society of the 21st century. Here I am not referring exclusively to class disruptions or addictions. Lack of affection, family problems, influence of the media, and peer pressures confuse many students and leave them disoriented. More and more new disturbing behaviors or fashions emerge and spread inside schools. One of them is bullying, which involves threats, mocking, continuous persecutions, fear, and pain, and it becomes increasingly sophisticated and dangerous due to the use of social media. What can we do? The absence of adults forces us to rely on experts. Zero tolerance policies and experts are important, but what is needed is true adults accompanying the youth. More than ever, adults are needed to truly educate the youth, to make them grow, and to give them hope.

The learning environment is favored when there is discipline in the classroom. In the presence of a vigilant teacher, students take the class seriously, respect the teacher, and respect each other. To this end, it is also important to foster peer learning, to catch students doing something good and to praise them, to favor student initiatives, and to prefer and empower students with a constructive attitude. For students it is crucial to discover that their peers and their teachers share the same interest for learning, that they are ordered and oriented in the same path, and that they are companions in the same educational journey.

Sports

Sports are an important part of American schools. Because of that, it is imperative that we not forget that sports are educational activities. We forget this when we downgrade them to entertainment or pastime, when they are not aligned with the school vision, or when they acquire such an importance that they become a burden for the academic life. In some cases, sports teams become so competitive that they establish their own non-educational goals, and victory or team become ends in themselves. Sometimes school teams manage big budgets and are stressed about recruiting coaches and providing scholarships to acquire the best players; in addition, players long for fame, success, and college scholarships. Such schools are not concerned about the misplaced focus because winning championships create a very important marketing tool and energize the school community. However, the fact that there are school teams exploiting their students because they want to win at any cost, and the fact that their players are more interested in becoming celebrities than in being educated are signs of the human and educational crisis that we discussed in the introduction.

To practice a sport is a very important educational activity; it provides education about life. Because of that, students who would like to practice a concrete sport and do not make the tryouts should not be deprived of the opportunity of practicing that sport. Schools should use their creativity to meet their needs. Students are introduced to the meaning of life through sports. In practicing a sport, the student commits to an activity that involves sacrifice, disappointments, mistakes, trust, obedience, self-control, passion, joys, friendships, and growth. Life involves all of that too. Sports practice is life practice. The goal of practicing a sport is to grow in knowledge of what life is about and to grow in self-awareness. The school wins not when the team wins, but when the players grow in self-awareness. This can happen both through winning and losing games, if school administrators and coaches understand the true meaning of practicing sports in school.

Sports practice fosters not only self-awareness but also team playing. In turn, team playing introduces students to a true knowledge of peers and rivals and of a true relationship with them. The student learns how to relate to peers, how to discover goodness in the other, how to work with them, and how to play rivals while respecting them. Team playing is more than socialization; it enables students to have an integral experience of unity with others in a society in which individualism dominates. This is a very important aspect of education, because team dynamics are similar to the dynamics in a family, in a classroom, in the workplace, or in a community.

The goal of practicing a sport is not to win or have success but rather to grow in fulfillment. When students are clear about this goal, then they can be engaged, use all their talents, give all their effort and sacrifice to win, and improve their skills, and they will always enjoy it and grow. Healthy competition is good. It is a way to test our skills with the skills of others. It is fair to desire to win and to put our energy into it. Our humanity always emerges when we play. Obviously, we have to respect the rules of the game; games have rules, and life has rules as well. There are so many factors involved in the game that sometimes victory does not depend on the player's effort or abilities, and sometimes the rival's abilities are simply superior. However, to lose games is part of life, and students can grow enormously on those occasions while learning from their mistakes and being provoked to work harder. It is an important educational goal for students to learn how to win without being proud and to learn how to lose without considering themselves losers.

A key aspect that we cannot forget regarding the practice of sports is the body. Over the last decades, a misconception of the body has spread. For many students, the care of their bodies has become a kind of cult. They do not like running, but they spend many hours in the gym, take substances to make their muscles grow, get tattoos, and follow strict diets. Sometimes they become obsessed or even sick, suffering anorexia. Part of the education that should take place through sports practice is the focus on an adequate conception of the human body. It is important to have healthy bodies and to exercise them, but at the same time, we have to be aware that our bodies are the home of our minds and our beings.

The coach is an important figure. Schools have to choose coaches who can communicate the school vision to the students through the practice of their sports. It is a great mistake to hire coaches who can be great professionals but transmit a concept of life and a worldview different from that of the school, because sometimes students follow the coach more than they follow their teachers or even their parents. All that was said about teachers and their role of transmitting the school proposal and the school vision applies to coaches as well. Coaches must foster not only the physical growth of the child or the improvement of his skills, but also his self-awareness and the growth of his humanity. A way to do it is to enlarge his longings. It is not enough for a student to desire to win games, to have a healthy body, or to get a college scholarship. I am not against that. However, the coach has to help them long for more, for the infinite. The coach educates students to expand their longings by helping them face difficult moments, grow in their capacity for sacrifice, and work with peers. To this end, the coach has to demonstrate his love for what he does, show them his fulfilled humanity, and invite them to live the same experience.

One of the mistakes that coaches make is to favor the best players and to neglect the least talented. Each player has infinite value regardless of his athletic talents. Each needs to grow as a human being. The coach has to educate with charity and provide special attention to all of them, just as parents do with their children or teachers with their students. A coach is a coach not only during the season but also during the entire year. Therefore, coaches should continuously monitor and foster athletes' academic and human progress. Initiatives such as study halls can support such vision.

The school gym and the school fields are places of good or bad education. The way practice is developed, the way facilities are taken care of, the way games are played, and the ways people cheer are all factors of either good or bad education. Games are great occasions for the transmission of the school vision. It is the responsibility of school administrators and coaches to be fully aware of that.

Diversity

Modern societies in the 21st century usually manage diversity following two main models of coexistence: multiculturalism and assimilation. For Oriol, according to multiculturalism, no cultural or ethnic group must prevail, all groups must have the same opportunities, and society is a mosaic formed by all groups. Pure multiculturalism implies relativism, in which there is total respect for diversity. Oriol points out that assimilation is a model in which there is a predominant or common culture integrating other cultural minorities to some degree. A pure model of assimilation might involve total uniformity and the loss of identities. For him, pure multiculturalism and pure assimilation have in common that both deny the possibility of a sincere dialogue among cultures in which there is openness to integration and, at the same time, true respect for diversity.[225]

Schools are part of this broad sociological context, but they must integrate all students regardless of their origin and build human coexistence inside a relatively small physical space. In our schools, we can find students from very different backgrounds, cultures, and socioeconomic levels. Many of them belong to the first or second generation of immigrants, and English is not their first language. They also have different learning capabilities. In addition, although teenagers usually follow the same fashions, they often have a tendency to rebel against authority and affirm themselves by trying to look different from the rest, sometimes even in foolish ways. Because of all the above factors, schools can become human explosive cocktails. It seems that – even after establishing adequate rules and receiving the help of psychologists, social workers, pedagogues and other experts – it is becoming more and more difficult to integrate students while respecting their diversity. Given this sociological context, how can a school deal with diversity and educate people who are different?

Cultures, in abstract, do not enter into dialogue, but concrete people do. What is needed, first of all, is to look not at what divides people but at what unites them. It is true that schools try to integrate people through common ideals and rules. However, it is the humanity in us that is inherently and originally common, universal, and unites us. In the fourth chapter, it was said that there is a universal human dimension. Every human being has the same elementary human experience: the same complex of ultimate questions and longings for love, truth, beauty, justice, and happiness. It is the recognition of the elementary experience of every single student or teacher that guarantees a true respect for his diversity. Therefore, the recognition of the elementary experience of the person we encounter – student or teacher – is the cement that builds true dialogue, coexistence, and unity inside a school.

Even students who belong to the same ethnicity or culture are very different from one another. They have different talents and abilities, different personal circumstances, different worries, and different tastes and expectations. However, all of them have infinite value and an infinite longing for happiness and fulfillment. A student or teacher who is aware of this is able to embrace the diversity of others – and also their incoherence, limit, or sorrow –, learn from it, and even use it as a resource. All of us have had the experience of helping or being helped by a person who is very different from us. At that moment, we saw the way the other person thinks, what he loves, and what he is, and, for an instant, we felt a kind of bond with him. This dynamic among students generates a sense of belonging to a special friendship and contributes to unity. In this way, in a school or a classroom, diversity can be turned from an obstacle into a motivational and instructional resource.

Parents

Research shows how vital the involvement of parents is for the success of students.[226] However, for various reasons, parents are becoming less involved than ever in the education of their children, delegating this responsibility to schools or even to grandparents. This situation is becoming more complicated due to the increased number of single-parent and broken families. The rising absence of the father's role and the increasing presence of stepfathers, stepmothers, and significant others in families is making the education of children more difficult and the parent-school partnerships more complex.

In light of this situation, what should the role of the school be? First, the school should help parents to become aware of their responsibility as primary educators of their children and should try to show them what the education of a human being entails. Second, the school should collaborate with parents and involve them in partnerships. Let us analyze the first scenario.

Family relationships are experiencing a cultural change. The parent-children relationship is increasingly becoming private, reduced to feelings, deprived from its mysterious nature, and dispossessed from the awareness that it implies a crucial task. What task? The most important task for parents is to communicate to their children a meaning of reality as a whole. Parents and teachers hand on to the youth the cultural patrimony that they received from their ancestors. They are the bridge that connects children with a rich past. For this reason, for the existence of this bridge, the past – with all of its hypotheses and its total meaning – can be interesting for children.

Parents not only are responsible for the growth of the child, but also for the continuity of the world. These two tasks are different and may conflict with each other: the child needs protection from the world, but the world requires protection from the potential harms that a newborn and a new generation can inflict on it, too.[227] We have the obligation to educate well so that new generations do not destroy themselves and the world.

What educates children is not only words but also a human experience that parents live at home and communicate to them. This does not exactly mean moral coherence or the absence of family problems; rather – as we said with teachers – it means ideal coherence, a kind of consistency about the meaning of things and the human being. Through the beauty of an experience lived at home that corresponds to their humanity, children obtain a sense of the world.

Parents do not educate alone. They connect with other people who share the same worldview and build an educational community. The complexities of our global world and of the struggles that children live during their adolescence invite parents to develop a network of relationships that helps them accompany their children.

Let us develop now the second role that a school should have: the development of partnerships with parents. Schools no longer have only the goal of educating children; they have to address families' needs as well. They must meet their social, economic, cultural, and educational needs, but they can also use families as resources. The school has to promote educational relationships among teachers, parents, and students. This way, all of them can meet each other, discover basic and existential needs, collaborate to satisfy them, and become educators of the rest of the school-community members. At the same time, they must become educated: more human and more aware of reality. The participation of parents in school life and school decisions is very important. There are parents who coach or chaperon after school activities or help with the preparation of school shows, fundraisers, and open houses. A good way to improve parent-teacher relations is for teachers to organize seminars once a year on a weekend, during which time parents attend as students and learn about subjects that might interest them such as astronomy, literature, or video production.

It is important for parents to become school partners from within their own homes. Parental involvement does not equate parents physically entering school facilities and supporting school activities. The majority of parents are busy during school hours. Others do not speak English or are afraid of meeting teachers or administrators. However, they can do many things from home: they can assist their children when they are studying or doing homework; maintain high expectations for their learning; praise and encourage them; help them to organize their time; use school learning materials with their children; discuss school matters with them; support school activities; encourage reading; and assist with proofreading.

The relationship between concerned parents and concerned teachers deserves special attention. There are teachers who would be very happy to get rid of some students and there are parents who would always act as representatives of children's unions. Here is John Locke's advice to the parent regarding the teacher: "You must be sure to use him with great respect yourself and cause all your family to do so too. For you cannot expect your son should have any regard for one whom he sees you or his mother or others slight."[228] A non-antagonistic attitude is important, but it is also crucial that they respect the responsibilities of one another, that they establish two-way communications, that they take into consideration the concerns that both parties have, and that they work together as a team.

Community

We have heard it said many times that it takes a village to educate a child. Schools form communities, are part of bigger communities, and belong to the society at large. No school can exist isolated. Students, teachers, administrators, families, businesses, local organizations, and local governments interact with each other and share interests. School-community partnerships improve not only academic success but also success in other areas. Sheldon showed that schools establishing family, community, and school partnerships increased student attendance.[229] A qualitative research of secondary schools from southern Ontario developed by Hands found that collaboration between schools, homes, and local associations enhances academic results and moral development.[230] However, a study by Epstein and Sanders in 161 schools, colleges, and departments of education (SCDE) confirmed that educators lack the skills and capabilities to develop partnerships.[231]

First, we have to ask ourselves, from where will they find the energy and the skills needed? Second, what kind of community is needed in the school? Third, what kind of partnership does the school need to establish with all of its external stakeholders to make its students more human? To answer these questions, let us go back in time to the Middle Ages.

Schools and universities are not an invention of government. They were born inside the fabric of society, from the free initiative of individuals and communities. In the Greek and Roman cultures, there were no schools for the public. Only the elites had private tutors or attended academies. When the Roman Empire fell in the fifth century and chaos governed Europe, monks such as Cassiodorus, born between 485-490AD, started copying classic manuscripts and, because of that, our culture was preserved. For centuries, their monasteries were places where the Western culture was preserved and transmitted to people, including the poor. Later on, in 1179, after the III Lateran Council, all cathedrals established free schools. Although they were not incredibly numerous, they provided free education to the public and constituted a big educational effort at that time.

To see the initiative of individuals in action creating educational communities, it is important to analyze the origin of universities. They were born as "universitas scholarium" (students' communities), "universitas magistrorum" (teachers' communities), and "universitas magistrorum et scholarium" (teachers' and students' communities). They were local associations registered as corporations or guilds. Particularly interesting is the case of the University of Bologna, established in 1180; it was founded by the free initiative of students, who were the managers and had the capacity to hire professors and elect the rector.

Our schools should be places in which this free and dynamic initiative of individuals and local communities, which is part of our tradition, is followed. They should be communitarian adventures. For example, teachers should be generators of community fabric. It is very important that they participate in the development of the school vision and school planning. Sincere dialogue is needed among them and with the school administration to help provide ideas, clarify questions, take ownership, build partnerships, and transform the vision into an experience that they live and share.

Another example is the student body. It is in the school, in a living reality, where the student has to test the proposal offered by parents and teachers. The proposal is a life lived to the fullest. In the friendship with other peers, with some teachers, and with parents, this proposal is tested. When students see that the proposal works, their fulfilled humanity expresses itself by acquiring a particular intelligence of reality that, through osmosis, is transmitted to their peers. These students – with more or less awareness – build the school community, build society, and build the common good, as did the 12th century students of Bologna.

Teachers, students, parents, and local communities may have frequent meetings of all kinds, without creating the essential school community or school-community partnerships. What is required to form a true community? The requirement is a reason to be together: a reason for educating and being educated. People need reasons to live. People need meanings for their existence and for the world. Schools are places where people use reason, seek truth, and find significance. When a teacher, a student, or a parent discovers the mystery and the piece of truth that is in the other, he discovers an indissoluble unity with that person. Through encountering this kind of people, a diverse companionship is generated. The school community builds itself and builds its unity through people who live and share this human experience.

Chapter 6

Curriculum

What would be the curriculum's main features in the school described in the fifth chapter? In what way would subject matters provide the education needed to overcome this human crisis and cultivate the students' whole beings? In what way would they foster growth in awareness of particular realities while simultaneously nurturing growth in awareness of reality as a whole? To this end, what kind of contents and textbooks do we need? Although we would need another book to fully answer these questions, I will provide some ideas about the curriculum and some of its disciplines that can help school administrators improve their academic planning. These ideas can also be useful for teachers to enhance their lesson plans and educational activities.

The goal of the curriculum and its subject matters is the development of the student as a human being. The curriculum is a hypothesis of meaning, a way to read reality, a map of reality. It is the proposal that the school offers to the students and that students have to personally verify. Students have to look at reality and see whether they are better able to understand themselves and the world from the inside of this human experience proposed by the school through the curriculum. The proposal – the curriculum – is presented to the students through subject matters.

Every subject matter is a view of reality, a road that leads to the discovery of a piece of the world, and each subject is a piece of reality that is explored with a powerful instrument: a hypothesis of the meaning of reality. Subject content is proposed to the student, allowing him the freedom to test it with the hypotheses offered. Meanings of concrete realities are discovered when the relationships of those realities are grasped – particularly the way they relate to the whole. The student grows because he is able to connect a particular content with its universal meaning. However, because every subject leads only to a specific part of reality, every subject has a strong and a weak point: on the one hand, it allows us to learn more about that particular reality; on the other hand, there is a risk of reducing it by disregarding its connection with the unity of knowledge and the totality, which is present in any reality.[232]

To avoid this risk and to avoid scientism, which consists of raising science to the level of ideology, we can follow two suggestions. First, every subject matter has to respect its own boundaries and methods. This way we avoid, for example, trying to explain human experience through mathematical demonstrations and chemical reactions, or literature through psychology and political ideologies. Second, every subject has to respect its terminology, vocabulary, classifications, and categories. Meanings are discovered through connections made between concepts, categories, and terms. Confusing terminologies result in a lack of connections or wrong connections.[233] For example, a cause, a reason, and a source are often used as synonyms, but depending on the discipline and the circumstances, each can lead to a different meaning.

Every subject matter should be transmitted in a simple and concise way and should include essential content that condenses the substance of the discipline and is clearly understood by the student. Essential content refers to the basic content required to live as authentic human beings. Such content will evolve along the academic path to more articulated structures so that the student is able to build his foundations and see the steps of the academic and human journey. Every step of the journey takes into account the essential contents and goals of every discipline; the needs of the students and their physical, intellectual, and existential growth; the interdisciplinary connections among subject matters that are needed to favor their needs and growth; and the unity of knowledge required to discover a clear picture of reality.

The goal is to grasp meanings, connect them with the universal reality, and comprehend the truth they carry. However, given that all disciplines are connected and complement each other, premature specialization – or fragmentation, multiplication, or omission of subject matters – leads to a distorted learning of all disciplines and impedes the student acquiring awareness of reality as a whole. The origin of this problem sometimes lies – as was said in the fifth chapter – in the fact that we confuse the dignity of subject matters (which is the same for all) with their importance and function (which are different), conceding to them the same academic value and hours of instruction and demanding from the students the same effort.

What has happened in our country during the last century is that many educators and reformers have suggested that it is better not to have a clearly defined curriculum. Why? According to Dewey, "Progressive education fails to recognize that the problem of selection and organization of subject-matter for study and learning is fundamental."[234] Additionally, many educators try to avoid traditional subject matter instruction, because they believe that it leads to "rotten" learning from the past. They believe that educators should not propose our tradition and the history of our civilization to the children. For Dewey, the view that instruction must "derive its materials from present experience and should enable the learner to cope with the problems of the present and future has often been converted into the idea that progressive schools can to a very large extent ignore the past."[235]

In some ways, these beliefs are still present in 21st century American schools. Hirsch has devoted a great effort to denounce the "anti-curriculum movement" and the animosity against setting disciplines: "The lack of a specific, grade-by-grade subject-matter curriculum in most of today's public schools suggests... abandonment of a coherent academic curriculum... abolishing traditional academic subjects."[236] Nonetheless, it is fundamental to offer something to the students. It is crucial to determine what we are trying to achieve. If not, it seems that we do not want to do it or we are unable to do it. Recently we have tried to solve this problem by becoming more serious about implementing standards. However, as Ravitch points out, "Our schools will not improve if we continue to focus only on reading and mathematics while ignoring the other studies that are essential elements of a good education."[237]

Finally, another risk that we have to face is the fact that political powers sometimes try to impose certain viewpoints and create loyalties through the definition of standards that specify the curricula's content and textbooks' configuration. Furthermore, they control the instruction of such content through standardized testing. First, a curriculum's content should never be a matter of political interest. Second, standardized testing should not lead teachers to "teach the test," devaluing curriculum and learning to what those tests can measure.

Textbooks

Our textbooks, readings, and other auxiliary materials have to be a help – not an obstacle – in introducing our students to the sense of reality. The content of a book should facilitate the student's growth in self-awareness and awareness of the world. Let us see some criteria for choosing the right textbooks.

Books should favor a historical-narrative style instead of the encyclopedic and analytical style that today's texts have. Narratives describe facts and their history, human experiences, and the processes and steps toward truth that led scientists to great discoveries. Students easily understand them and can make parallels with their personal lives. Instead, today's textbooks try to provide large amounts of information displayed through data, graphics and complex analysis, showing abundant formulas that are deprived of their historical origin and using complex and technical vocabulary that students cannot understand or relate to their lives.

According to Postman, "Most textbooks are badly written and, therefore, give the impression that the subject is boring... knowledge is presented as a commodity to be acquired, never as a human struggle to understand, to overcome falsity, to stumble toward the truth."[238] In his opinion, most textbooks have no human personality and foster trivial learning and dogmatism.

For mathematics and science textbooks, it is interesting what Freudenthal suggests: teaching and learning should be implicit in the book; in other words, the process should be stamped into the text. The goal is "to have users reinvent the educational development that produced the textbook as though they had participated themselves in its production process; and by users I mean both teachers and learners." He also suggests including meta-questions on the textbook such as: What do you think? Did I ask you? Why do you think? Did I supply you with this? Did I claim that? Did you learn in...?[239]

Books should also portray the human dimension. To choose adequate texts, we must compare the content of the text with our human experience and see if they picture, clarify, deepen, exalt, and educate it, or if they disregard or confuse it. "History books – says Ravitch –reduce stirring events, colorful personalities and riveting controversies to a dull page or a few leaden paragraphs. Read the literature textbooks with their heavy overlay of pedagogical jargon and their meager representation of any significant literature."[240] History textbooks usually fail to discuss biographies of key figures of our history; science textbooks disregard the lives of scientists and the history of their accomplishments; and literature books dissect poems and novels, killing their souls and depriving them of the powerful feelings that they stir. Textbooks substitute all of that for impersonal analyses such as sociological interpretations, arid formulas and demonstrations, or complicated definitions and terminologies.

Textbooks should be simple, have essential content that synthetizes the discipline, and be fully studied. Every book provides a view of reality. Given that it is impossible to include everything, the challenge is how to choose its content. However, by including some contents and excluding some others, the picture of reality changes. The majority of textbooks are big and expensive encyclopedias, but they methodically disregard certain topics. All of them look the same, because apparently they follow certain standards. Teachers should not be confused by the apparent objectivity of these texts. They should choose small books that offer appropriate selections of essential contents required by standards, and complement them with their own notes. Plato reminds us, "The voice of the master is far more decisive than any book."[241] Taking notes also helps the student understand that learning is not acquiring a ready-made knowledge but rather is something that happens in a dialogue with the teacher and his peers. Furthermore, taking notes helps the student to be attentive and engaged in the class discussion, assimilate what is discussed, and personalize it with his own words.

At this point, the reader might be curious about how this kind of education can be implemented through the various disciplines. The reader might like to see examples or might wonder how mathematics or chemistry relates to the particular human experience of a student. For this reason I will choose some subject matters and offer ideas that people can use – especially administrators and teachers in their instructional planning – to cultivate the humanity of the youth and introduce them to reality as a whole.

Mathematics

Mathematics is like a good novel. There is an intriguing plot, marvelous settings, and fascinating characters that awaken intense feelings in us such as curiosity, excitement, awe, sacrifice, frustration, beauty, satisfaction, and joy. With adequate teaching and learning, mathematics can educate the students' whole beings and can be a stirring exploration of reality.

However, for various reasons, this is not what usually happens. First, mathematics is not easy; it follows a progression in which the student discovers new knowledge using knowledge previously acquired. Second, it demands personal work: the student has to learn a method and take ownership of it to investigate reality. Third, it is usually taught in a reductive or fast way that is not appealing to the students. They associate mathematics with difficult formulas, calculations, and a huge set of abstract rules. For many students, it equates failure and disgust. Because of its utilitarian use, mathematics has been reduced to mechanical calculus; its true nature of intuition, creativity, and rationality are forgotten. This is what happens when teachers give students definitions and rules and tell them how to proceed; and when learning is reduced to the memorization of theorems and formulas that are disconnected from their process of discovery. Thus, in the end, it becomes something boring, rigid, and dead.

The starting point for the student should be this question: How does mathematics relate to me? The answer to this question is found in our tradition, in our history. That is why the history and developments followed in mathematical discoveries should be taught with their respective theorems. Rudimentary algebra was born in the Orient around 4,000 years ago, and modern mathematics, in particular geometry, was developed in Greece almost 2,500 years ago as answers to problems that humans had. During the 17th century, analytical geometry and integral and differential calculus were developed by scientists as ways to explain physical phenomena. Mathematics and science progressed generation after generation by means of people adding further understandings of reality to that which they received from their ancestors.

Today, as in the past, reality approaches us and allows itself to be known; and humans long to find reasons to explain it. For this reason mathematics has to be a human experience, something alive and dynamic; it must be the experience of having intuitions, making connections, discovering truth and beauty, and finding answers that allow us to solve problems and lead us to new questions. Now the challenge is how we should teach it to provide the student with this experience.

According to Freudenthal, the answer is not a mechanical training following a deductive, ready-made system but rather "an activity"; a "guided reinvention" of the learning process that mankind followed throughout history. In other words, students have to reinvent the mathematics that they have to learn with the help of the teacher. "The learner should reinvent mathematizing rather than mathematics;

abstracting rather than abstractions; schematizing rather than schemes; formalizing rather than formulas; algorithmising rather than algorithms; verbalizing rather than language." And what should the student mathematize? "This can be answered in one word: Reality."[242] He believed that students should find their own levels of exploration by receiving as little help from the teacher as each case allows. This way, learning is more motivating; mathematics becomes a human activity; and skills and knowledge, being acquired in an autonomous way, are more readily available and better retained.[243] We could summarize it by saying that mathematics becomes something that relates to the student.

After a weekend, students do not remember much about what they studied the previous week. Why? It is because they did not understand. There is a strong connection among learning, understanding, and memory. For Donovan and Bransford, "Learning with understanding supports knowledge use in new situations."[244] But why did they not understand? It is because they were not truly involved or interested; because of that, they did not take ownership of their learning. Part of this human activity of reinvention is creativity, observation, and intuition. Another part of this human activity is mistakes. In fact, important mathematical – and also human – actions are to spot our mistakes, to find their causes, and to overcome them. To learn from our mistakes is crucial for our growth in mathematical knowledge as well as for our personal growth.

Mathematical laboratories are a good way to experience, to act out, and to invent this subject matter. They generate contexts in which the student actively participates by searching for meanings and answers, involving his whole person (reason, affection, even his body), and taking ownership of the method used and the knowledge discovered. The fifth chapter emphasized the importance of a classroom concept similar to that of a repair shop in which father and son explore and work together, and the son learns by actively seeing how things are made. Math labs can be developed inside the classroom with the type of awareness that one would have in that kind of repair shop. In a math lab, students can receive a problem and be asked to develop group work. Students can identify hypotheses and use manipulatives, mathematical instruments, software, and other technologies. This dynamic is very useful for students to learn how to elaborate questions, listen to different viewpoints, and receive feed back from the teacher and other peers. At the end of the activity, each group can verbalize the steps followed in the problem's resolution. A lab activity for 6th graders could be to measure the longitude, surface, and volume of different objects in the class by inventing their own measuring system. This lab could continue by asking the students to measure the entire school with their measuring systems.

Something crucial that students must learn is that abstraction is the power of the human being, because it is the capacity to read reality, to extract its meaning. The student can interact with abstract realities that are different from the ones that we perceive with our senses; and by doing so, he can grasp the meaning of material realities. "The birth of modern physics – says Whitehead – depended upon the application of the abstract idea of periodicity... this would have been impossible, unless mathematicians had already worked out in the abstract the various abstract ideas which cluster round the notions of periodicity." He affirmed that the same was true with trigonometry: the more abstract it became, the more useful it was, because it was better able to explain other physical phenomena.[245] We understand reality by describing it, by representing it with our reason, by coding it and decoding it with the help of models, and by improving our models. The model of a particular reality is not the absolute truth of that reality, but it is a guide to understanding it.

Another key aspect of teaching and learning mathematics is its language and verbalization. For Freudenthal, verbalization thrusts abstraction: "Horizontal mathematization leads from the world of life to the world of symbols. In the world of life one lives, acts (and suffers); in the other one symbols are shaped, reshaped, and manipulated, mechanically, comprehendingly, reflectingly; this is vertical mathematization."[246] Mathematics has its own language, and it is very important to learn it. When the student is able to narrate –speaking and writing – the process followed with reasonable explanations, he becomes aware of it, and mathematics becomes part of his personal life. If the student is not able to do this, it means that he did not understand, and it is better not to move forward. Therefore, it is important to demand order and clarity, and to correct the way mathematical expressions are conveyed by using the appropriate terms and definitions or by always including the units when results are offered.

However, the starting point cannot be the language – learning by heart definitions, formulas and theorems – because this would reduce mathematics to deductive and automatic learning. It takes more time, it does not provide quick results, and it is more difficult for teachers, but adequate math learning implies that students must follow intuitive and creative critical thinking. The teacher should not provide answers, formulas, or the steps to follow but rather should introduce meta-questions that indicate alternatives and examples that engage the student's sense of reason, lead him to additional questions, and, eventually, guide him to reinvent the whole process. For example, a demonstration should not be a memorization exercise but rather a process in which the student uses his reason and asks the truth to appear before him; then, using his intuition and logic, he is able to predict and show how the truth will reveal itself.

To this end, it is far more educational to provide word problems for the students than to give them numerous exercises to mechanically solve. A problem requires a great deal of observation. It is important to carefully read the text and scrutinize all data. That problem, that particular reality, can be observed from many different perspectives, but the student has to choose one and elaborate a hypothesis. At this point it is very important to pay attention to the goal of the problem, what he has been asked to find. The goal helps to identify the hypothesis. Then the student may or may not find the right answer, but he will be able to describe the process, many questions will be born in him, and he will lose the fear of facing new problems.[247]

This way of learning mathematics corresponds to the longings for truth, beauty, and fulfillment of the student's humanity. It stimulates the search for truth. Mathematics does not consist of opinions. When facing a problem, the student interrogates reality and develops hypotheses that he will eventually verify. By doing so, as an event, truth suddenly will show up. The same process can be followed with existential problems. Acquiring this habit, the student not only will pass the class but also will grow in certainty about mathematics and about life. "Those who discover a mathematical truth look at it as an artist looks at his work... seems to be a work of beauty, when different concepts and properties come to fuse marvelously in a superior harmony of number and forms."[248] When the student discovers truth, he has an unforgettable experience of satisfaction. Beauty and fulfillment are the fruits of a work: the rational process that leads to truth.

Interdisciplinary connections are crucial in introducing the student to universal reality. We arrive at a better understanding of reality through the study of various disciplines, finding relationships among them. That is why it is very important to open every discipline to the knowledge of the other. This is easy in the case of mathematics, because mathematics permeates physics, chemistry, economics, and also art and music and the rest of the disciplines. Roger Bacon said that "Without four sciences it is impossible to know the rest... and the door and key of these sciences is mathematics."[249] In fact, mathematics is the language of science, and it gives science its capacity for coherence and a considerable degree of certainty that it would lack alone. Teachers can establish many relations between mathematics and other subject matters. For example, high school geometry allows for the exploration of many physical phenomena and realities that can lead to interesting connections with physics. But at the same time, if we want to know what lines, numbers, and points actually are, we need more than mathematics.

Finally, students should become aware of the mysterious nature of mathematics. I would like to emphasize the close connection between mathematics and the idea of totality, or reality as a whole. De Giorgi, famous for solving the Hilbert's 19th problem, says about the mysterious nature of mathematics that even if we want to focus on finite processes, we have to follow procedures of an infinite nature: "For example, an addition of two integers is an operation that is done with a limited number of steps, but to define the addition one is forced to speak of the infinite totality of natural integers."[250] Along this line, it is important to highlight the definition of 0-dimensionality, by which every single point can be isolated from the rest and encircled in a region of space that can be made as little as we want.[251] Both the Archimedean number π and the number e, whose discovery was published by Euler in his *Introductio in Analysin Infinitorum*, have a mysterious and infinite nature. We also have to mention the fact that modern mathematics is built around the concepts of limit and function, and it is still in continuous evolution. For many years, nobody could prove Fermat's Last Theorem, but in 1994, Andrew Wiles did it. Moreover, there are many problems still open, such as the Goldbach conjecture.

However, mathematics becomes really mysterious for students when we explain to them that a large proportion of the concepts that we teach them are not as immutable as we tell them. The discovery of non-Euclidean geometry proved that the axioms of Euclid were not valid as the mathematical structure for physics. Einstein, describing how the theory of relativity changed Newton's theory and had to provide new laws of gravitation, showed his astonishment as follows:

> "The path was thornier than one might suppose, because it demanded the abandonment of Euclidean geometry. This is to say, the laws according to which solid bodies may be arranged in space do not completely accord with the spatial laws attributed to bodies by Euclidean geometry. This is what we mean when we talk of the "curvature of space." The fundamental concepts of the "straight line", the "plane", etc., thereby lose their precise significance in physics... The new theory of gravitation diverges considerable, as regards principles, from Newton's theory."[252]

This does not mean that the Euclidean geometry has no use. For small distances there are no significant differences between Euclidean and non-Euclidean geometry. Furthermore, without the discovery and development of Euclidean geometry, it would never have been possible to discover non-Euclidean geometry. We build models to explain reality, but we always depend on something else: on the willingness of reality to allow itself to be known.

Science

Many of the ideas provided in the previous section could be useful in this one as well, because the challenges that teachers and students face in mathematics and science are similar. Many times the way science is taught and learned is by processing large amounts of information and abstract concepts. Sometimes science is reduced to ready-made sets of information or exercises in which students apply formulas and follow deductive procedures given by the teacher. Students might use the right formulas and solve the exercises without really learning the science itself. In these cases, students are not truly engaged in learning because they do not see connections between those formulas and the real world, and among the specific content discussed on a given day and the previous lessons. Furthermore, when science lessons are linked to the real world, it is done to show its technological applications, not to facilitate the student to gratuitously become aware of nature and find its link with his existence.

To study science means to study nature, to encounter nature. Even if its appearance is sometimes chaotic, it is always attractive, interesting. Students are particularly attracted to the study of the nature that surrounds them. That is why in science, it is important to emphasize the inductive method because it allows students to move from the observation of the facts and natural realities around them to their generalization in universal concepts. For the student to be able to follow this process, teachers have to educate their reason in an integral way – by means of introducing them to the scientific method – and must provide them with a unifying view of the universal nature. Scientific knowledge always tends to provide global explanations, but, without a unifying hypothesis, the student is unable to integrate the concepts that he learns.

How can learning science be an integral and human experience? By observing nature with our students, we all are educated in the concepts of truth, goodness, and beauty.

When we patiently, attentively watch nature, it approaches us and reveals its truth. We are educated in the concept of goodness when we perceive that there is night and day, and seasons, and a mysterious and providential reality in our planet's very specific conditions for us to be able to exist. The beauty and order of nature leaves us in awe when we look at the stars, go to the top of a mountain, see the sunset, observe animals and plants, or study the human body. The study of certain issues such as the human body, the cosmos, or the concept of evolution can easily obtain the existential involvement of our students in class. It is also easier to engage students when we study science history, practice the scientific method, or make interdisciplinary connections. Let us develop these three topics.

Science history introduces us to the human dimension of science. The compassion that Einstein showed Newton when he discovered the theory of relativity and had to develop new gravitational laws shows us that scientists are human beings. Our students can identify with them, with their humanity, and with their curiosity, passion, mistakes, and challenges. This is what engages students in learning: to experience that they are developing an important task in life with those who have gone before. This is also the context in which the history of science should be taught. Instead of teaching it in chronological order, on tables with data about their accomplishments, we should frame the concept studied in the historical context of a particular scientist. For example, when studying the transmission of fluid-pressure, we talk about Pascal, his humanity and challenges, the questions that he asked nature, the process that he followed to arrive at his law, and what he learned about life through all of those studies. Pascal is an example to follow. Science is an amazing river of humanity that flows along history and invests us with its fascination. The challenge for us, when studying very specific contents with our students, is to not lose the unifying vision and the infinite horizon of nature that the greatest scientists had.

The second topic that I want to discuss is the scientific method. Our students have to learn the scientific method to know how to interrogate nature and follow the right steps that, hopefully, will lead them to know it. A good way to introduce this topic is to invite a scientist to the school and let the students ask him questions about his work. We have to show our students the importance of an observing and questioning nature, and then how to collect data and try to identify relationships and signs of repetitiveness. These relations and signs will lead us to develop and test hypotheses and models with which we will try to come up with a better understanding of the particular phenomenon observed. However, it is important to show our students that every phenomenon is a sign of another reality; it relates to other phenomena. We must simultaneously show them that they need a guide, somebody who educates their reason because he sees more and because he has a passion for witnessing how reality unveils itself.

We should make our students aware of what science is and what it is not. Some scientists, moved by different ideologies, state the absolute truth of some questionable arguments, elevating science to the level of ideology and turning science into scientism. Others, trying to infuse skepticism, affirm that science is relative and is a matter of opinion, which is not true if we follow a true scientific method. We must also make our students aware that without the proper use of reason, it is impossible for science to embrace reality. Also, modern research imposes so many restrictions on how scientific investigations must be developed and on the goals that they target that no room remains for knowing reality as a whole.

Finally, it is important to discover with our students the connections between science and other subject matters. The goal is not to establish automatic interdisciplinary links among subjects but rather to help our students grow in their unifying vision of reality. Science is a method for humans to read reality. However, natural phenomena must be translated into a language for human beings to understand each other and continue the investigations of one another. This language is mathematics. Another important connection to discuss with our students is that of science and ethics. We have to remember what Rabelais said: "Science without conscience is the ruin of the soul."[253]

A good interdisciplinary approach to the natural world is the study of environmental science, because it links physics, chemistry, biology, geology, geography with studies related to the atmosphere, ecology, or engineering. What is important is to not downgrade it to its pragmatic technological applications or to ecology. It should be a place where students openly explore and contemplate with amazement the immense and astonishing nature. There are teachers who take their students on field trips to show them forests, mountains, and waterfalls; others even grow a little botanical garden.

Now I would like to provide some ideas about teaching and learning physics, biology, and chemistry.

Physics

Some teachers are able to develop many experiments in class, and others cannot. Regardless, students are generally able to repeat some abstract definitions and formulas or mechanically develop some experiments. However, very often they do not know how to observe the physical reality and ask questions. That is why they have to learn the scientific method by putting small experiments into practice. The point of departure of this method is always facts, concrete realities, and experiences, not lectures. And then, from those concrete realities, the teachers help students generalize and form conclusions regarding the concepts. We can present phenomena familiar to them, such as electricity, magnetism, heat, or movement. Then, they can collect data, formulate a hypothesis, and try to develop a model, an explanation of the phenomena. Finally, they can present the results of their investigation and become familiar with concepts, formulas, and definitions.

In this context, we have to introduce them to the history of physics and the models that have tried to explain the physical reality along history. Physics cannot explain all physical reality, but we can develop models that explain some aspects of it. Models in physics are not exactly the same as models in mathematics. No model in physics has been absolute, because all of them either became obsolete or were improved. However, models are useful because they help us understand reality; hence, they are valid instruments until we find better ones. We have to talk to our students about Newton and classical mechanics: how he discovered gravity from Kepler's laws of planetary motion, how he invented the derivative and infinitesimal calculus, and how centuries later, his studies allowed us to put artificial satellites into orbit. Then we have to discuss magnetism and scientists such as Faraday and Maxwell and how they introduced the doubt about classical mechanics. Finally, we have to study all of the developments of quantum physics and its authors: Planck, Einstein, Bohr, Schrödinger, Heisenberg, Pauli, Fermi, etc. We must also discuss the way they saw those developments, as Schrödinger explained:

> "Einstein told us that energy has mass and mass is energy; in other words, that they are one and the same. Now the scales begin to fall from our eyes: our dear old atoms, corpuscles, particles are Planck's energy quanta. The carriers of those quanta are themselves quanta. One gets dizzy. Something quite fundamental must lie at the bottom of this, but it is not surprising that the secret is not yet understood.[254]

Matter is an important topic to discuss with our students. As Schrödinger points out, matter is a complex mystery. The solid appearance of visible matter confuses us, making us think that it is reality. However, the most recent discoveries show that matter is an undetermined "something" that is infinitely analyzable. Beyond electrons, quarks, and neutrinos, there exists undetermined cosmic "stuff" or energy. What is fascinating is that matter organizes itself in such an incredible way that it can host the human body, the human mind, and the human spirit in what we call "the human being". The student is able to reason and love because this undetermined cosmic "something" provides a body for him.

We should also emphasize the study of the universe, its order and laws. This way we may have a foretaste of a superior and mysterious beauty, as Sagan said: "Contemplations of the Cosmos stir us – there is a tingling in the spine, a catch in the voice, a faint sensation, as if a distant memory, of falling from a height. We know we are approaching the greatest of mysteries."[255] We may make a historical introduction. Since the antiquity, the human being has observed the cosmos with awe and infinite questions regarding meaning. We can continue with the Greeks and arrive at the Middle Ages and Copernicus and the analogy between the cosmic order and creation's order. Then, we study Galileo, Kepler, and Newton; and we finish with the space exploration age from the Sputnik to the Hubble. The student can identify with the awe, curiosity, and search for truth that so many different people showed throughout history. Students will have an unforgettable experience if, instead of presenting a documentary in class, we make a field trip to a planetarium or watch the stars with them at night. They grow because the amazing observation of this mystery causes in them an integral involvement.

The following activities can awaken great curiosity in students. The first one is to compare the dimensions of some objects with planets and galaxies and then to compare the distances between planets with the distances between stars and galaxies. The second one is to encourage a discussion about the particular conditions that allow Earth to host life. Many events took place apparently by chance to produce those specific conditions. The third one is to discuss the origin and the expansion of the universe, matter, and antimatter. There is a great mystery involved in this, because although we can know many things that happened after the Big Bang, we will never know what happened before the Big Bang. As T.H. Huxley, one of the greatest advocates of Darwin's theory of evolution, said, "The known is finite, the unknown infinite; intellectually we stand on an islet in the midst of an illimitable ocean of inexplicability."[256]

What follows is a demonstration of how a topic could be studied using an interdisciplinary approach. Light, with its particles and radiation, can be studied as a physical reality. A star and a bulb issue light. This mysterious reality was historically considered a metaphysical reality. We can study its speed, which is very high but not infinite. That is why when we observe very distant objects, it is as though we were looking back in time. We can study light in relation to geometry if we make a light ray pass through different layers of water, glass, and air. The ray changes the course of the light, creating different angles. We can also study light in the context of the arts, such as the way painters produce lights and shades in their works or the way architects create luminous spaces.

Biology

In this section I will refer to the different disciplines that could be included under the umbrella of biological sciences. Because biology, in general terms, deals with a broad range of knowledge, the challenge is to choose the appropriate aspects to study. The textbook usually makes this selection, and because biology textbooks are big manuals, the risk is to turn the class into the transmission of too much information that students will have to process in disgust.

Given the progress that research has made in this field over the last decades, teachers do not usually discuss biological history. It is not my intention to encourage its chronological study. However, as stated in previous sections, it is important for the student to identify with scientists, follow the steps that they made, and try to interrogate nature the way they did. An example of a horizontal approach to biological history is to study together the origins of cell theory, evolution, and genetics, three important topics in biology. While Hooke discovered the cell, it was in 1839 that Schwann developed the cell theory and stated that cells were the basic unit of life. In 1859, Darwin published *On the Origin of Species* stating that evolution comes from natural selection. In that time period Mendel developed a study of thousands of pea plants that led him to the formulation of his genetic laws.

In the biology class, it is more challenging to find ways for students to apply the scientific method, but teachers can help them become familiar with the school's environment and develop appropriate experiments. The goal is for the student to interrogate nature, to follow an inductive method. We cannot begin the class by presenting definitions; it must be the opposite. There are always plants, animals, insects, or even forests close by. When possible, we need to take the students there. First, students have to observe and analyze the environment in which they live; they have to describe what they see and collect data. Then they can gather samples and take them to the classroom. This activity always engages them, because every living thing contains a secret, and it is their job to discover it. I always wonder why students get so excited when they dissect animals; it is because they want those secrets to be unveiled. When it is not possible for students to physically see certain animals or plants, we can show a documentary. From the study of concrete realities, describing their properties, we move to the generalization of those properties and then onto categories and definitions, paying particular attention to the technical vocabulary. After that, we can develop an experiment. Then, from the study of the living reality as a whole, we may move forward, studying its parts. Finally, from the macroscopic level, we may descend to the microscopic one.

The living world is complex and can be studied at different levels: molecules, cells, living realities, and ecosystems. Any creature can be studied from all of those perspectives. For this reason, we must always follow a global approach and pay attention to the environment in which that creature lives. The student has to be able to interrelate the different levels and understand the living reality in its context.

Some important topics that we should discuss with our students are the extraordinary phenomenon of life, evolution, and the human being.

Everybody takes for granted that the origin of life was spontaneous. We have to allow our students to ask themselves open questions such as: Why does life exist? Is it because of an accident? Why does life reproduce? Is there any purpose for life? Life is an exceptional phenomenon. The very fact that life exists, that there is a place in the universe for the human being, and that I exist is flabbergasting. The extraordinary properties of the Earth, such as its chemical composition, location in the universe, and plate tectonics, among others, show that our planet is not a compact ball of dust spinning around but a home that makes life possible. We have to make our students aware of this and encourage discussions in which existential questions arise. The more we know about the order, beauty, and mysteries of nature, the more nature demands a global explanation from us.

Although it is impossible to discuss evolution in a paragraph, here are some thoughts:

- Biological evolution, understood as Darwin's theory and the later research that expanded it, is an authentic scientific theory.

- Ideological interpretations of evolution try to explain all reality (including the human spirit), imposing a materialistic view of the world, reducing human beings to their biological element and denying the possibility of the existence of formal and final causes. We have to remember that the research method has to be imposed by the object studied and not ideologically imposed by the subject.

- Not everything in nature can be demonstrated: the scientific research of nature does not prove the existence, or the non-existence, of final causality. However, reason submitted to experience determines that teleology (formal and final causes) exists.[257]

- Chance does not coincide with mechanistic determinism and must be seen as part of the dynamism of nature and part of the mystery of the universe. When discussing this topic, it is important to study not only Darwin's theory and new developments of evolutionary theory, but also the history of paleontology and important paleontological discoveries. Students must know the facts and learn how to formulate scientific hypotheses, avoiding preconceived notions. Open questions should be favored as well.

Another crucial topic to discuss is the human being, who is a very particular creature. First, begin the study from the perspective of man as a transcendent human being with a mysterious nature that is aware of the cosmos. Man is complex, with his unity of body and spirit, freedom and reason. Man's body has an incredible harmony and extraordinary complexity. It is impossible to reduce the human to biology and psychology. Second, study the different parts of the human body without depriving them of their dignity by presenting them as pieces to be assembled. Refer students to the functions and actions of the person, and always discuss them in the context of the human being as a whole. For example, connect the study of the eyes with the complex function of vision in which the eyes and brain are linked to the experience of a person who sees things and becomes aware of them. Third, from the macroscopic study of the person we can descend to his microscopic study, but always referring to him as a whole being.

In this context, the person's sexuality can be studied. Sexual education is usually reduced to the study of anatomy, psychology, prevention of certain diseases, and contraception. However, it is fundamental to study sexuality in the context of the human being's mystery and his extraordinary importance in the universe. This topic is a great occasion for teenagers' growth if they study it by reflecting upon their existence. Here are some ideas that teachers might want to discuss:

• Sexuality is a dimension of the person.

• The adolescent matures and some developments happen.

• The human being cannot live alone and has infinite longings for love and fruitfulness.

• It is crucial to love the freedom and the destiny of the person loved.

There are far more mysteries involving the human being than what many textbooks offer. John Eccles, Nobel Prize winner for medicine, had a notion of the person not reduced to only biological substances and psychological perceptions:

> "There is a great mystery in our existence and in our life that is not explicable in materialist terms... we are creatures with some supernatural meaning as yet ill defined. We cannot know more than that we are all part of some great design."[258]

Chemistry

This is clearly an experimental science. Chemistry creates the things it has to study. This discipline in particular cannot be taught as a collection of abstract concepts because the experiment plays an important role in the learning process. Above all, it has to be an experience lived through the mastery of the scientific method. This does not mean mechanical activities should be developed in the lab, but rather, that students should observe phenomena and substances familiar to them and study their properties. In this manner, they can experience chemistry by seeing, touching, manipulating, and developing small experiments.

For example, if we want to discuss the concepts of water and air, we can ask students to measure humidity, temperature, and atmospheric pressure over different days. They can process the data and compare the weather conditions of those days. Then they can boil water and see how it evaporates. We could connect this activity with the study of weather in geography class. Other examples could involve the observation of different materials and their chemical reactions. Students can conduct easy experiments in which they see substances reacting. They can perceive them boiling and producing smells, heat, or even fire. The goal is to make students experience some phenomena and after that, to ask them to conceptualize what they observed. Then we can move from the macro perspective to the micro, studying what is inside the matter: molecules and atoms.

If we begin in the opposite direction – from the micro view and going to the macro – students will not be as engaged, they will think chemistry is abstract and boring, and they will not experience reality or acquire direct knowledge of it. Therefore, it is not appropriate to study what is inside the matter without having observed the matter and studied its properties. Some teachers may look at this method as something more complicated or even disordered. It is true that it takes more time than it takes to present some definitions or formulas on the board. It is true that some procedures and organization must be provided. However, if teachers discuss this method with their students and explain to them the reasons they follow a certain path, then students will be more engaged and will enjoy experiencing chemistry.

The way chemistry was born and developed makes it easy for students to connect its contents and models with their history. Students should become familiar with the life of Lavoisier. While trying to find the composition of water, he discovered the conservation of mass, which is how modern chemistry was born. In 1794, during the French Revolution, a judge sentenced him to be guillotined, stating that the Republic did not need scientists.

An example of how we could introduce specific content, with its history, and how we could link chemistry with physics is the following. Before discussing the periodic table and atomic theory with our students, we can explain to them that molecules are the smallest units in which substances can be divided while conserving their chemical properties. Then we clarify that atoms form molecules and ask them to form structures representing molecules. After that, we can introduce them to the lives of Proust, Dalton, Mendeleyev, and Rutherford. Proust discovered the law of definite proportions in 1793, which is the foundation of analytical chemistry. In 1803 Dalton, while trying to explain Proust's law, discovered atomic theory. In 1869, Mendeleyev created the famous periodic table with the 70 elements known at that time. By displaying all chemical elements according to their atomic weight, he found a pattern of characteristics and further developed his table by leaving empty spots for unknown elements that he was sure would eventually appear. In 1911, Rutherford discovered the structure of atoms.

Here is another way that we could engage our students when discussing chemical reactions, especially hydrolysis. We could connect chemistry with literature, economics, environmental science, and biology. We can start by reading the passage of *The Mysterious Island* in which Jules Verne explains how water, through its decomposition (hydrolysis), would be the coal of the future. Then we can discuss the high price of oil and its impact on the economy. After that, we can talk about pollution, global warming, and the need to find new, clean, and cheap energy. Later, we can discuss the double decomposition reaction, pointing to the fact that, being reversible, it produces energy in one direction and consumes it in the other. Then we can show that hydrolysis can be catalyzed in a process similar to the way enzymes work in the digestion process. Finally, we can have an open floor discussion about the importance of energy and the tremendous respect that we should have for it. Energy is a universal good and a scarce commodity. We depend on energy, and it is our responsibility to ensure that new generations will enjoy it.

Language

Language is a fundamental instrument that human beings use to know reality. The Greek word "logos" means two things simultaneously: "word" and "reason". Human beings establish relationships with things in order to know them. Using their reason, they assign words to things. Words are symbols of things. A greater understanding of reality develops when we are able to express our thoughts in articulated sentences in writing or in speaking. Using language, we establish a relationship with the world and understand it. Using language, we see the links that events, people, and things have among them and with us; this is how their meanings reveal themselves. Because of that, language should be an important goal in all subject matters, and all teachers – not only language teachers – should foster language proficiency.

As children grow up, they gradually develop their capacity for abstraction and learn to articulate sentences while being aware of their meaning. At the beginning, they use words that identify and describe concrete objects. Then, they are able to use abstract concepts, such as loyalty or freedom, and they enlarge their reason to grasp meanings and elaborate thoughts. This happens not only with the primary language but also with mathematics and science. As we discussed in the previous section, math and science are languages; by learning these languages, the child learns how to read reality. The child translates phenomena into scientific or mathematical language, and then he translates those formulas or axioms into his primary language.

The question is, how can language be a guided discovery and an integral experience? For all of the concepts stated above, language learning cannot be downgraded to boring grammar lessons, morphological-syntactical exercises, and vocabulary drill. Language teaching is about educating students' reason to nurture and enhance their language experience. This cannot be done through lecturing rules and doing mechanical exercises, because we cannot separate reading from reality and from the person reading it. Vocabulary, grammar, syntax, or morphology have to be discovered by students while they are engaged in real language experiences: reading, writing, listening, or speaking. The student learns how to use the language correctly by using it.

We teach students how to write to help them learn how to reason and how to express what they see and learn. Furthermore, in learning how to write and speak, the person understands himself as well as reality. A person knows how to write when he is able to synthetically grasp his experience. This happens when he is able to unify concrete details; when he is able to witness the way things and details assemble themselves through his words. The more a person develops this capacity, the more he is able to perceive what lies behind the appearance of reality. To this end, we can follow the same method of "guided reinvention" that we discussed in mathematics. For example, we may read a text with our students and ask them to identify the theme and indicate what the author is doing (describing, criticizing, etc.) and how he is using the language to do it. Then, we may ask them to create a similar text with a similar theme and using a similar style and syntax.

A good way to develop writing skills in our students is to encourage them to create a school newspaper. Under the guidance of teachers, they can search for truth, beauty, and goodness in daily school life; then, when they find them, they can express their opinions about them in writing and share them with the school community.

It is very important for students to learn grammar. Without knowledge of how to use words appropriately, they are not able to express what they see, what they think, how they love, what they want, and so on. However, grammar must be learned in concrete contexts. It is important that students write by describing things, developing critical thinking, and reflecting upon themselves. It is good for them to write about things that they know or have studied. After the teacher has corrected their work, it is important that they rewrite it because grammar is also learned when texts are analyzed. The student has to learn how to interrogate the text: what is important; how it was developed and what the syntax and morphology are; what the key words are, what their meaning is, and how to classify them; what the role of simple sentences is in a particular paragraph; and what his opinion about the text is.

English is a language with many roots, and its vocabulary is derived from many different places. An engaging way for students to discover the English language is through the study of its history, which is the history of English speakers and how they integrated and developed their language by assimilating words from other languages.

In reference to language speaking, Piaget, Vygotsky, Chomsky, and many others have studied the development of language in children. Language development, in particular language speaking, is essential for the development of our students' humanity. We should make our students speak, but not only for them to acquire some skills or to test whether they understood the lesson. The goal of language learning is the student's change. When the student expresses his thoughts, he is ordering them as he speaks, and thus, he understands them better. This can be easily seen when the student talks about his personal challenges. While talking about them, he reflects upon them, and he grows in awareness. This also has an effect on his peers. The more articulated he becomes, the greater a chance there is that his peers will become more articulated and aware of themselves as well. There are different ways to foster speaking: developing dialogues or persuasive debates in class; asking students to develop short speeches about different topics; reading out loud; or enacting short plays.

Finally, I would like to mention the importance of mastering foreign languages. English is the second language of almost every major nation. However, this is not an excuse for Americans to learn only English. The study of foreign languages helps our students to understand other cultures, to understand how other people live, love, and think, and to acquire a better picture of the world as a whole. Unfortunately, foreign language teaching is often very poor and downgraded to grammar and exercises. Our students should have the same full immersion experiences in foreign languages and cultures that children have when they are born. They should be constantly exposed to the language in all four dimensions (reading, writing, listening, speaking). However, we should put the emphasis on making them speak so that they gain confidence in themselves. To maximize their learning, it is also crucial to use authentic materials such as conversations, online newspapers, music, maps, and restaurant menus. They should develop cultural projects in which they learn the country's social life, history, art, geography, or gastronomy. Finally, assessment in foreign language should include oral interviews.

Literature

Literature, more than any other subject matter, records the human condition and causes it to emerge. The human being has passions, questions, thoughts, furies, and challenges. Literature registers in words all of that, all that is part of being human. However, good literature is more than feelings; it transpires the truth of the human condition, the mystery of the human condition: its existential questions and its longings for love, beauty, truth, goodness, fruitfulness, and fulfillment.

To read is to dialogue with an author, with his experience of life, and with the way he conveys it. The author makes daily circumstances sublime, filling small details with the meaning of the infinite. The author, by sharing his experience, provokes a jolt in the reader's humanity, makes it emerge, and at the same time clarifies the reader's experience, and makes him understand it. This is the goal of the literature lesson: to impact the student's humanity. If the lesson attains this goal, the student will be excited about discovering the sense of certain words such as love and freedom, experiencing what those words mean, and knowing more about the author and his works. In addition, all of that will engage him even more and will make him eager to scrutinize the book and find out more about the plot, settings, characters, and style.

However, this does not always happen. Many times teachers do not focus on the author, on his existential search and experience; rather, they prioritize other aspects. They disconnect the text from its dramatic events, from the author, and from reality, and therefore, from the student.

They are experts in providing technical information, dissecting and killing texts, developing impersonal, abstract, and cold analyses of linguistic structures and styles, and infusing sociological ideas. However, if the text is dead, who is interested in it? Some teachers are not even interested in great authors. They prefer that their students read many mediocre authors so that they can better entertain or indoctrinate them. Students end up being bombarded with many authors and non-essential information, and therefore, remembering very little of it.

In the literature class, it is more important for the student to see the teacher moved by reading a play or a poem than to receive information from the teacher. The most important task for the teacher is to allow himself to be moved when the whole class is filled with awe by reading a paragraph together. Later, the teacher must witness to them how his humanity has changed after reading that paragraph. His students, by osmosis, will imitate him, and when they are later reading books at home, they will realize that their humanity has changed. The student forms his own method of reading and writing – many of which exist – by imitating his teachers and the authors that he reads.

This also applies to the criteria we use to choose books and reading selections. We have to be aware that the majority of our students do not read much. They surf the Web or read fantasies, but they do not reflect on what they read. Thus, here are some ideas:

- It is better to thoroughly read a few significant books written by great authors than to read many pieces of mediocre books.

- Students should read the classics because they develop essential themes and have been able to enlarge the humanity of men throughout the ages.

- The type of reading, style, and theme should correspond to the age and needs of our students. Sometimes students have reading difficulties. In these cases, I would suggest tailoring literature texts to their interests and abilities just to get them reading, gradually increasing the challenge.

- Readings should include literature that has been important for the transmission of our tradition and for the development of our civilization.

- Books that portray the mystery of the human condition are important.

- Readings should help students make interdisciplinary connections and relate them to reality as a whole.

For middle school, I would recommend, in particular, epic books. They engage students by awakening noble ideals, narrating entreating adventures, describing ancient cultures and their values, and making readers walk in the shoes of heroes. Particularly important are the lives of our founding fathers and those who made our nation great; important protagonists of world history; and classic epic books such as Homer's *Odyssey* and *Iliad*, Virgil's *Aeneid*, and the medieval romances of *King Arthur*, *Chanson de Roland*, and *Cantar del mio Cid*. Depending on the reading abilities of our students, we may either use the original versions or shorter adaptations with easier vocabulary. By reading these kinds of books, the student can identify with the characters and ask himself the same existential questions that the characters asked themselves. Especially important is Ulysses, *Odyssey*'s main character. The student can accompany him in his trips and face Poseidon's storm, sirens, Polyphemus the Cyclops, and the enchantress Circe, and can experience love for Penelope, Telemachus, and his homeland. *Ulysses* is the title of a great poem by Alfred Tennyson, as well as the book by James Joyce, in which Bloom finds the strength to go back home with his wife and start anew his life.

I would encourage the reading of great American and British authors. Given that teachers are usually familiar with them, I am not going to mention them here. I would ask teachers not to forget Shakespeare. He makes the human condition emerge in an incredible way: dramatic, sublime, full of life, and passion. He makes Romeo and Juliet say, "I am you and you are me," showing that true love is total unity. He depicts forgiveness in the *Merchant of Venice* and pride through *King Lear*. In *Macbeth,* he portrays ambition, describing how the heart of man develops self-examination. Often his characters are full of contradictions. He demonstrates the journey of life and shows how, through dramatic circumstances and tragic events, truth arises. He does not give ready-made answers to human longings; rather, he leaves existential questions open.

In addition to the American and British classics, I recommend the following works and authors because they can help students grow in self-awareness and awareness of reality. Starting with novels, I would mention Dostoevsky's *Crime and Punishment* and *The Brothers Karamazov.* Dostoevsky's characters are usually "thirsty". Nothing can satisfy them. They deal with goodness and evil, and desperation, but above all they express a longing for hope and mercy. Flannery O'Connor's writings permeate humanity, make us experience the mystery in the daily circumstances of life, and challenge the notion of the human being and the world that our media conveys. For Spanish classes, I would recommend short adaptations of Cervantes' *Don Quixote*. Explaining the parallelism that exists between the life of Don Quixote and the life of Cervantes can enhance this work.

Regarding poetry, I would suggest works that do not devalue this genre to sentimentality. Dante's *Divine Comedy* is one of the world's great pieces of literature. It is a literary journey much different than the one of Ulysses. This is the journey that leads the person to his fulfillment. Dante introduces himself as the true Ulysses. Guided by Virgil, he develops a journey of knowledge, from darkness to the encounter with Beatrice and with the truth of himself. In his journey, he sees history and all its developments and famous characters through the eyes of a fulfilled person, the eyes of eternity. Another great Italian poet is Leopardi. His works offer much more than feelings; they offer a view of the human. In *Dominant Thought,* he expresses man's need for a total answer to his longings. In *Thoughts*, he shows the disproportion before the total existential answer. And in *The Portrait of a Beautiful Lady,* he evokes the mystery of the human being by showing how beauty creates desires for the infinite. Additionally, I would suggest some poems: Milosz's *Meaning*, Whitman's *Grand is the Seen*, some Shakespearean sonnets such as *Sonnet 25*, and Ada Negri's *My Youth.*

Finally, I would like to emphasize the importance of encouraging our students to read and enact plays or fragments of them. When students act, they experience the value and transcendence of certain words, the significance of pronouncing them in public, and the impact that they have in our hearts. In addition to Shakespeare and other great Anglo-speaking and American authors in general, I suggest the following plays because they can help our students grow in self-awareness. *The Tidings Brought to Mary* by Claudel depicts life as a calling, showing how love generates the human and generates a people. This view of love is not the expression of feelings but rather is true and selfless donation. Milosz's *Miguel Mañara* tells how a Spanish noble man changed from being an incredible womanizer to become a true and exceptional human being. The change happened when he encountered the gentle Jerónima, who stands out to him because she is not like the others he had known. When she dies three months later, in the midst of his sorrow, Miguel experiences the call to a new life. Finally, I would suggest an excerpt from the fourth scene of *Caligula*, by Albert Camus, in which the Roman emperor, agitated, argues with his counselor because he wanted "the Moon, happiness, or immortality" but could not obtain them. This piece reflects the longing of all humans for the infinite.

History

Learning history means to see the past coming back to life before our eyes, to be struck by dramatic events, and to understand them in their global context. History is the encounter with the human experience of men and women. Entering a relationship with that experience, we discover an important part of our identity, because those events belong to us and help us to become aware of who we are and where we come from. Herodotus, the father of history, defines the discipline in the first sentence of his *Persian Wars* in the year 440 BC in the following manner:

"These are the researches of Herodotus of Halicarnassus, which he publishes, in the hope of thereby preserving from decay the remembrance of what men have done, and of preventing the great and wonderful actions of the Greeks and the Barbarians from losing their due meed of glory."[259]

High school students tend to hate history, classifying it as "boring". This often happens because learning history is downgraded to the memorization of dates, names, and battles. Textbooks provide abundant chronological information but not many narratives through which the student can easily understand the richness of important events. Additionally, history education in school is fairly recent. It began in the 19th century and was greatly influenced during the 20th century by the French journal *Annales d'histoire economique et sociale*, which provided a particular view of history. It put the emphasis not on leaders or events but on sociological and economic factors, social groups, and mind-sets. This was not bad in itself. In fact, the *Annales* tried to correctly interpret events by creating a science, not wanting history to be a list of names without critical thinking. It is true that to understand a particular historical event, it is important to know the society in which it took place, including the people's mentality and their economic circumstances. However, the point of departure for some historians is not a sincere desire to research the facts but rather a prejudice or an ideology such as Marxism or economic liberalism.

Following this approach, many textbooks, consciously or unconsciously, deprive history of its vivacity and reduce it to a chronological evolution of ideas. When teachers follow these dynamics, they do not help their students to use critical thinking or learn the historical scientific method. Students are not challenged to observe people's lives and objective facts, interrogate them, and form conclusions. They are obliged to memorize information and ready-to-wear sets of ideas. Furthermore, this way of teaching history does not consider the subject of knowledge –the student – and does not provide a method to learn the object of history, which is the past.

How could the study of history be different? How could it become a human experience? Here are some suggestions. First, it is important to select essential contents. If students have to learn a huge chronological list of items, what is conveyed is that all of them have the same importance, and none of them are remembered. Also, events happen not only chronologically but also synchronically. This means that sometimes different events happen simultaneously and one can greatly influence the other. We just saw this phenomenon recently during the Arab revolutions of 2011. Teachers should distinguish between secondary facts and transcendental events, which imply important developments and have crucial consequences for the course of history. Teachers should identify those essential events and study them in depth, establishing a dialogue with the leaders who were involved and the decisions they made; not devaluing them to naïve interpretations; and connecting them with other crucial events that happened at the same time and in other moments of history.

Consciously or unconsciously, there is no neutral teacher of history. That is why the teacher's viewpoint and his attitude about life are crucial. The history class will be an experience for students, and that experience will depend on the teacher's worldview and personal human experience. The teacher must choose between presenting a chronological list of information or trying to search with his students for what people throughout history have considered true, fulfilling, and human. We cannot disregard the importance of the discipline's contents in student motivation: the discovery of substantial truths and examples of truly fulfilled people is what engages students the most; it is also what makes them grow in knowledge of the world and in self-awareness. Teachers should also help them to connect those substantial truths with their personal interests, needs, and lives.

Meaning is vital in teaching and learning history. In understanding the meaning of important events in history, one can understand better his life, and present events and can face the future with more awareness. However, knowledge of history depends on the interpretation of the meaning of concrete human actions. More important than discovering the facts, it is to understand them. Therefore, it is more important for the teacher to help the student revive history and grasp its meaning than to explain facts. Thus, the teacher helps the student to use his reasoning skills to interrogate those facts, listen to what the protagonists of history wanted to communicate, and grasp the motives for their decisions and the reasons certain events happened.

Teachers cannot be satisfied when students are able only to repeat the sequence of some events or provide the answers that they want to hear. Teachers should encourage students to use their reasoning skills, creativity, and intuition to understand the meanings of events and the relationships among them. To this end, open questions should be favored, and students who arrive at creative or unexpected answers by correctly using critical thinking should be praised.

After investigating an event, students should be able to develop a synthetic narrative of it. This task will be easier if the teacher uses comprehensible language and avoids excessive abstractions and technicism. It is also useful to have students practice in class and to give them assessments that include both written and oral narratives. A narrative is not a linear, abstract sequence of multiple facts but rather is the exposition of some essential facts in such a clear way that their meaning is easily grasped. In a narrative, there is an introduction, subjects, actions, developments, motives of those actions, results, and corollaries. A narrative helps students to remember important events and to place them in the appropriate period of time and with their main protagonists and nuances. It is also important that students know where the events took place. For this reason, history and geography cannot be isolated from one another. Maps and fundamental geographical contents must accompany narratives.

Another significant factor in history is the human dimension. If we want to educate and build true human beings, we must teach them history, because part of their identity is the history to which they belong. There is no history of ideas, as some teachers or textbooks claim. There is only the history of concrete people, the circumstances they faced, the decisions they made, and the facts that occurred. We can understand past events because they reveal to us how people were at that time, what their human experience was, and their notion of the human being.

The methodological mistake that some teachers and textbooks make is that they fail to emphasize the study of events, the people involved in them, and their cultural, social, and historical circumstances, all of which are necessary to arrive at the correct interpretation of those events. Instead, they reduce vital events, rich narratives, and the human dimension to abstract structures. Those structures try to simplify and generalize people that share similarities but are different; therefore such structures do not help but rather complicate. They depict a cyclical view of history and permeate a kind of historical determinism in which men's decisions are supposedly predetermined by previous causes and sociological factors. Therefore, relationships between events are reduced to causes and effects. However, men are not like stones; men have freedom. We cannot ignore that Western civilization has its roots in Greece and in a notion of the human being based on reason and freedom. The result of ignoring such issues is the loss of the human dimension, the loss of history's richness, and its degradation to sociological or, even worse, ideological interpretations.

The points of departure for this method are Marxist, liberal, deterministic, or economic premises. Teachers or textbooks use them to arrive at prejudiced interpretations of history; these may be ideological-economic, deterministic, or even based on race or nationalism. Such interpretations were clearly seen during the 19th century and are what makes vibrant events seem to be cold and abstract facts. This makes it difficult for us to connect with the men who lived those events and to understand their human experiences, which is why history is not attractive to students. This manner of teaching history makes its learning difficult, because students are unable to connect the abstract concepts and ideas with their own lives.

Teaching history this way also makes it difficult to preserve the richness of our civilization or transmit it to the new generations. Until recent years, the memory of the past was very important for the development of civilizations. However, a distorted idea of progress has neglected its importance. Without knowledge of the past, we do not have the meaning of our present or (even less) of our future. It is impossible to disregard our history. When we are born, we are born from two people, in a family, in a people. We can't know a person if we do not know his history; we can't know a people unless we know the society's history; we can't know ourselves if we do not know our history. History is the memory of peoples. We need to know our history, because when we are aware of our past, we are more aware of our present, and we understand ourselves better. Thus we can also enrich what we have inherited, transmit it to the new generations, and plant the seeds for our future. In this manner our identity matures, our civilization matures, and our certainty in the present is transformed into hope for the future.

Students could revive history by reading the works of the greatest historians throughout the ages. Textbooks usually include interesting quotes from key figures and historians. However, it is better to read entire pages, letters, speeches, or manuscripts – depending on students' abilities and needs – in order to experience a full immersion in crucial events. Here are some examples of essential historical works:

- Herodotus of Halicarnassus, *Histories*

- Thucydides, *History of the Peloponnesian War*

- Chinese "Historical Records", also known as *Shiji*

- Livy, *History of Rome*

- Tacitus, *Germania* and *Histories*

- Julius Caesar, *Gallic Wars*

- Augustine, *Confessions* and *City of God*

- Procopius, *Polemon*

- Gregory of Tours, *Ten Books of Histories*

- Cassiodorus, *Variae* and *Institutiones Divinarum et Saecularium*

- Ibn Khaldun, *Muqaddimah*

- Marco Polo, *Travels of Marco Polo*

- Christopher Columbus, *The First Voyage*

- Niccolò Machiavelli, *The Prince*

- Alvar Núñez Cabeza de Vaca, *Relación*

- Sir Thomas More, *History of King Richard III* and *Utopia*

- John Locke, *Two Treatises of Government*

- Robespierre, *Speech Promoting Execution of King Louis XVI*

- Napoleon Bonaparte, *Correspondence of Napoleon I*

- David Livingstone, *Missionary Travels and Researches in South Africa*

- Winston S. Churchill, *His Speeches*

- Mikhail Gorbachev, *Speech Dissolving the Soviet Union*

Regarding American history, it is impossible to specify in a single paragraph the most important works and authors. However, students should read crucial documents such as the Mayflower Compact, the Declaration of Independence, the Constitution (particularly the Bill of Rights), the Monroe Doctrine, the Gettysburg Address, the Corollary to the Monroe Doctrine, and the Truman Doctrine. Students should become familiar with the works and/or speeches of key figures of United States history such as Benjamin Franklin, Thomas Jefferson, George Washington, Abraham Lincoln, Roosevelt, John F. Kennedy, Martin Luther King, Jr., and Ronald Reagan. They should also familiarize themselves with writers such as John Smith, John Winthrop, Davy Crockett, Ralph Waldo Emerson, Henry D. Thoreau, and Nathaniel Hawthorne.

Finally, it is important for us to help our students grow in their capacity to read the signs of the times. The fall of the

Berlin Wall was a clear sign in history. Is this event connected with previous and later events? If we pay attention to history, we must acknowledge that there is a mystery behind it. Sometimes things happen for reasons that we do not understand. Other times events seem as if they are guided in a good direction for no apparent reason. There is always a mystery involved in history. When we see big dark clouds in the sky, we get an umbrella because we know that it will rain. With human actions and history, it often happens the same. The more attentive we are to the signs in reality, the more we can foresee certain events. The more we grow in humanity, the more we are able to perceive those signs and the mystery behind them.

Economics

Many students consider this discipline difficult and abstract. They acknowledge that it is important, but they believe that it is too complex. I do not blame them, because textbooks encourage a kind of teaching that disregards the student and does not provide the method with which the student can investigate and obtain knowledge of economic realities. Economics textbooks are influenced by the same abstract structuralism and determinism that we discussed in the history section. Teachers usually follow those textbooks and transmit to their students abundant information, complex graphics, and abstract definitions. Some students take this subject matter seriously, because they believe that it will help them make big money in the future. The problem is that some teachers believe it, too. On the first day of an economics course, we must provide an accurate definition of the discipline and explain what economics is about. If not, we will further confuse our students.

The best way to define this subject is to note its etymology. The term economics comes from the Greek "oikos," which means home, and "nomos" derived from the verb '"nemoo," which means "to administer". Therefore "oikonomia" is the ability to administer and lead the house and the household. From its etymology, we learn that economics is not about how to become rich but rather about how to manage our homes and the resources that we have, including our time, to the best of our ability. When provided with this definition, students are usually surprised, because they discover that economics relates to their lives and is not so difficult to understand.

This should be the way teachers teach this discipline: from the concrete to the abstract, from the particular to the universal. For example, if we want to discuss the markets, we should not start by providing definitions. We should start with a case study, comparing two pizza companies, for example. We introduce the topic with questions: What do they sell? What do they have in common? How do they compete? Do they compete with other companies? If I start my own business selling pizza at home, could I compete with them? What would my difficulties be in competing with them? When students grasp the concept, then we can start discussing markets in general and introduce other concepts, such as demand and supply. A similar example could help us to discuss competition and barriers to entry as well.

If we want to discuss the global economy and international finance, we can introduce the topic by asking the students what they believe countries exchange. They will suggest goods and services. Then we have to give them suggestions, such as what happens if your father works in Germany for three years? Where is that salary annotated, and which country is benefiting from it our country or Germany? Through this method, they discover that the movements of factors also modify the exchange among countries. At that point, we can simulate the trade between the two countries, and they can try to annotate the transactions and develop the accounting. After this exercise, we can introduce the concept of balance-of-payments account. The following week, we can proceed with questions that might help them see the relationship between exports, currencies, and interest rates. Thus, from the particular, we will arrive at the universal, and from the examples to the graphics and definitions.

It is crucial to help students distinguish between what economics is and is not. When we watch the news, read the newspapers, or talk with friends, it seems that everybody knows a lot about the economy. Our students must learn to differentiate between scientific information and speculations. Furthermore, they must learn the difference between positive and normative statements. Positive statements can be tested. They come from real data and scientific research. They are the result of the test of a hypothesis, and they might be part of a model that has been developed to explain economic phenomena. However, normative statements cannot be tested. They deal with what ought to be. The problem is that politicians and journalists intentionally mix real data with political maneuvers, confusing both statements and raising economics to the level of ideology. It is good to develop debates in class in which economic news is discussed. It is usually difficult for students to understand this type of news, so prior to those debates, students should observe data, establish hypotheses, and exercise their reason to draw some conclusions. Those debates help them to learn from the work of their peers. They also help students to distinguish between political economy, which is scientific knowledge obtained from economics, political science, and sociology about how a country is governed; and economic policies, which are concrete economic actions that governments implement (and that might be questionable).

The most important component of economics is the human being: his needs, his desires, and the decisions he makes. However, this component is the least studied and the least understood. This is why teachers usually do not cover this vital aspect in their courses. The way economic research is developed forces us to measure everything and to translate it into mathematical language. Because human desires and needs are difficult to measure, researchers either do not study them or reduce them to mechanic dynamics. What happens when we reduce the desires of human beings to technical analysis is that we are unable to understand them.

A clear understanding of human longings and human nature is fundamental to understanding economic phenomena. Because we lacked that understanding, we were unable to foresee the crisis. Financial markets, banks, and their regulation went wrong, but our capacity to understand our wounded humanity went wrong first. Now people wonder why there is no trust in the markets. As I said in the introduction, this is not an economic crisis; it is a human crisis. Therefore, the economics class should dedicate an important portion of its time to studying how human longings influence the economy. To this end, I would suggest the study of some important authors of the history of economics and some key contents of economics from the human point of view.

I would invite teachers not to forget to lead their students in the study of the life and works of the father of economics, Adam Smith. I would suggest reading Adam Smith's *The Wealth of Nations* as well as his *Theory of Moral Sentiments*, in which he discusses human nature, how men are driven by desires, and how they use their reasoning skills to deal with them. I would also suggest that teachers teach about the Great Depression and about John Maynard Keynes, reading his *General Theory of Employment, Interest, and Money*.

Now I would like to suggest some content and how we could discuss it with our students from the human point of view: labor; government size, debt, and the principle of subsidiarity; business and entrepreneurship, savings and consumption; common good, and solidarity; globalization; financial markets; and economy and environment.

Labor is defined in the economics class as a factor of production. It is usually studied in the context of human capital, workers' rights, and job market. However, it is, above all, a human longing. Péguy, in *L'argent*, says:

> "Those bygone workmen did not serve, they worked. They had an absolute honor, which is honor proper. A chair rung had to be well made. That was an understood thing. That was the first thing. It

wasn't that the chair rung had to be well made for the salary or on account of the salary. It wasn't that it was well made for the boss, nor for connoisseurs, nor for the boss' clients. It had to be well made itself, in itself, for itself, in its very self. A tradition coming, springing from deep within the race, a history, an absolute, an honor, demanded that this chair rung be well made. Every part of the chair which could not be seen was just as perfectly made as the parts which could be seen. This was the selfsame principle of cathedrals... The work was there. One worked well. There was no question of being seen or of not being seen. It was the innate being of work which needed to be well done."[260]

This human longing can be compared to the longings that we have for truth and love. Thus, we can say that labor is a human longing that leads to our fulfillment as human beings. The drama of not having a job is not only that we do not have a salary but also that we do not find an answer to that longing. That is why there are always many psychological implications associated with unemployment. When we study labor, it is very important to not reduce it to the contingent product of human actions; rather, we must always include the human being as the labor's subject. This is the most important dimension of labor; it is what provides its dignity and prevents us from distorting its meaning. Therefore, we have to discuss why labor is the most important factor of production, why labor is a need and a fundamental right for all men, why government and society must promote this right and create jobs, and why women cannot be discriminated against. In this context, we should discuss workers' rights and the unions' role. In this context, we should also discuss the need for an educational system in which the human dimension of students is educated. This is the only possible way to develop true human capital.

Currently, there is a big debate about government size and public debt. We need to discuss free market, the government's role, and the principle of subsidiarity. Free markets are one of the foundations of our economy. They regulate our economic system by producing and assigning goods and services in an efficient way. However, government intervention is needed to prevent and fix market failures. The welfare state developed for this reason. Nevertheless, increasing government expenditures and public debt growth cause us to consider ways to continue providing the services needed while reducing costs, trying not to increase taxation, and trying to be fair with the next generations. We should discuss with our students the principle of subsidiarity and how in some places there has been a successful reduction of government size, while strengthening public services. The principle of subsidiarity regulates relations between government, private sector, and society; it reduces bureaucracies and public expenses; and it strengthens public policies by encouraging businesses and non profit corporations to produce public goods and services. We should also discuss with our students the differences between subsidiarity and federalism or privatization. The result of federalism very often is the delegation or transfer of bureaucracies. Privatization sometimes can be reasonable, but at other times it provides big benefits to some companies yet worse services for the citizens. Through case studies, we can show how this principle leads us to the welfare society.[261]

Another important aspect to discuss with our students from the human point of view is business and entrepreneurship. Fruitfulness is a human longing. This longing is a powerful engine that encourages us to build families, houses, and businesses. Starting a business not only provides a profit but also creates employment and wealth for others. An entrepreneur betrays his humanity when he focuses his attention only on the profit and disregards the rest of the factors involved instead of seeking harmony among all of them.

When we discuss savings and consumption in class, we should emphasize the importance of making rational, human decisions. People, especially the rich, can greatly influence the economy through their decisions regarding investment and consumption. A wrong conception of money and its uses stems from a wrong conception of the human being and how to fulfill our longings. It is clear that wealth ostentation and exaggerated consumption do not provide fulfillment. At the same time, investments and consumption are needed to keep the economy moving. That is why we must discuss with our students ways to make reasonable economic decisions to balance the economy, preserve resources, and to be responsible human beings.

At this point we should introduce the concepts of common good and solidarity. No person can be fulfilled on his own. We need others, and we cannot be fulfilled if we close our eyes to the people who suffer in our midst. Solidarity is a human longing, but this human longing is not satisfied if it is devalued to mere feelings and does not arrive at a level capable of understanding the other and sharing his needs. This dynamic also happens at the social level. When two or more people are aware of this need and share it, they are building the common good. When human beings observe the needs of others, they use their creativity to provide answers to those needs, thus building the common good. The common good is the social answer to the longing for solidarity and fruitfulness that people have. Just as individuals can never be fulfilled if they pursue only their own interest, a society cannot be fulfilled if its members pursue only their own personal interests. In this same way, the government must pursue the common good; seek harmony among the interests of the different sectors, groups, and communities; and try to alleviate poverty. The government must favor the charitable action that many local communities and non-profit corporations develop to help people in need and build the common good.

We should not base our discussion of globalization, financial markets, and the economic crisis on mechanistic and deterministic interpretations, as if economic events always depend on strange cycles and confusing dynamics. Rather, we must study them from the perspective of human nature and the concrete decisions – right and wrong – that individuals, politicians, bankers, and entrepreneurs make. We have to emphasize that financial markets must be adequately regulated and must serve the real economy. At the same time, we must emphasize that the growing interconnection among economies compel the governments of all countries to correct the damages that globalization provokes and foster the benefits that should be produced by pursuing global economic and human growth and solidarity among generations and among the nations.

Finally, we should discuss with our students how important it is to promote global economic growth while preserving the environment. Many natural resources are scarce and cannot be reproduced. No cost-benefit analysis can be done without taking into account the extraordinary importance of protecting our planet and guaranteeing that new generations will enjoy living in it and using its precious resources.

Art

Art is a path of knowledge. Art is a language that, without words, describes reality in a creative, deep, and powerful way. Art also gives us a method to establish a relationship with the world that allows us to know it and to know ourselves. Through art, the whole emerges and manifests itself in a tiny but mighty reality. We are in awe when we discover that a piece of art is a sign of something greater, something exceptional. Images and other human creations are powerful signs of the essence and mystery of reality. The student has to learn this language, has to learn how to read these signs. Art invites the student to grasp what is hidden behind a painting or a sculpture, leading him to a human experience that is simultaneously mysterious and fulfilling.

In his novel *Demons*, Dostoevsky says that mankind "can continue without science, can continue without bread –it is only without beauty that we cannot continue, for there will be nothing at all to do in the world! That's where the whole secret lies."[262] Man cannot live without beauty. In this particular moment of history in which the dominant mentality and the media seem to favor the display of ugliness, horror, death, violence, and virtual images rather than the beauty of reality, art has an important mission: to allow beauty, especially the beauty of the world and the beauty and goodness of the human being, to emerge. Art awakens existential questions, makes us aware of what it is to be a human being, and restores our humanity. The beauty of art awakens in us desires for the infinite and for goodness, truth, and love.

Teachers should not surrender to the temptation of destroying the souls of art pieces by substituting the awe that they provoke for long, boring, and abstract explanations. When teachers prefer to dismember works of art, their autopsy, full of information about techniques and sociological ideas, will never be able to engage students' humanity. It does not work to teach art by teaching techniques that students have to apply, because students do not take ownership of those techniques or believe that art has anything to do with their lives. The proof of this is that they are not able to recognize those techniques in other works and are not engaged.

I do not mean that students do not have to learn art techniques at all. They have to learn some essential techniques, but they should learn through the encounter with artists and their works. In the art class, it is more important that students meet artists and their works than that they study for the sake of learning techniques. What engages students' humanity is to see the teacher's passion for art, the passion that the artists had for their works. The artist might be dead, but a dialogue with him is always possible. The artist usually shows an aspect of reality that we do not see. Sometimes the artist portrays reality in its truth, in its mysterious depth, and helps us grasp it. To meet an artist is an encounter with a passion, with a human experience. Students should dialogue with them, discovering their lives, their talents, their techniques, and their humanity. Teachers should invite artists to the classroom and, when this is not possible, should take their students to museums. A museum is a visual banquet. Obviously, it is impossible to see everything in a museum, so teachers should make a selection of essential and exceptional pieces of art and expose their students to those.

Once they are standing before a piece of art, students have to patiently dialogue with it and observe it the same way that the author did. Students have to wait for the beauty of the work to captivate and draw them; wait for the details of the work to merge themselves and show their meaning; wait for the humanity of the artist to emerge through that piece of art; and wait for the event of discovering the connection between their human experiences and the author's experience. Staring at a piece of art, the student makes it his own; he penetrates its soul and understands the reasons why the author created it, the technique that he used, and the steps that he followed. At this point, the student is able to revive the author's steps to redesign his work or another piece of reality. Then the student is able to recreate the work, using the same technique or modifying it with the technique of another artist or his own imagination; thus, he becomes able to produce his own piece of art.

It is important that students create their own works. They can start by developing a draft. This will help them envision all of the details of the work, steps to follow, materials needed, time and effort necessary, and technique or knowledge learned in class that should be used. The student has to express himself and shape his work according to his own talents, temperament, creativity, and particular view of looking at reality. The goal is to help the student to express himself and to enjoy doing it. The student's humanity grows in the process, particularly his longings for beauty and fruitfulness. Furthermore, through the creation of his own work, he will discover his capacity for sacrifice and his ability to infuse life into objects; he will learn from his mistakes, and he will learn to trust the teacher. He will be able to see his creation as a sign of the whole; he will be able to interpret other symbols; and he will marvel at the existence of any thing.

When the student cannot produce his own work due to a lack of time or talents or because of a lack of resources at school, the teacher has to help him to use his gaze. Whether producing his own work or struggling to do it, the student has to engage his own person, his reason and, in particular, his gaze. He has to pay attention to the proportions, perspectives, light, shades, contrasts, forms, colors, and other details. For example, light has been a powerful instrument for artists throughout history. Many centuries ago, it was only an intuition; today it is a complex technique, not only in paintings but also in fields such as architecture. Another detail of paintings is the use of people's gazes. In the paintings of Masaccio or Piero della Francesca during the 15th century, we can perceive how they involve the spectator in a dialogue of gazes in which the painting's characters show aspects of reality that he might not otherwise have noticed. Thus, these painters introduce the spectator to a more in-depth knowledge of the meaning expressed by the painting.

Regarding art history, we have to be cautious because some historians and textbooks try to emphasize a cyclical, abstract, and deterministic history to state that art follows stable and objective laws. They try to find common characteristics that create different periods, so that they can *a priori* apply them to art works and classify them. Thus, they avoid works that do not clearly depict those characteristics or do not follow them at all. However, those characteristics very often establish a cold distance that separates the student from artists and their works.

Having said that, I would like to highlight the importance of introducing students to the history of art. Modern and popular forms of art absorb students; few of them are consumed with a sensibility for classic art. This prevents them from obtaining the knowledge that classical art is able to transmit and from being influenced, through osmosis, by the incredible ways that artists throughout history expressed the magnificence and splendor of our humanity. It is fundamental that they become familiar with essential pieces of art in ancient civilizations: the Greek and Roman cultures, the Middle Ages, the Renaissance, and so on, finally arriving at modern art. Students must meet great artists of our history such as Giotto, Masaccio, Leonardo da Vinci, Michelangelo, Caravaggio, Velazquez, Rembrandt, Goya, Monet, Van Gogh, Picasso, Hopper, and Gaudi. Some projects can help students compare different art expressions in various epochs. A way to do it, for example, might be to compare how the human body has been represented throughout history. This activity can help students compare the notion of the human being and of the human body that men had throughout history. Although there are clear differences among these notions, all of them share a pattern, the need for beauty, truth, and goodness.

Notes

[1] Albert Einstein, *Ideas and Opinions* (New York: Three Rivers Press, 1954), 51.

[2] Phillip Blond, "Subsidiarity," *Traces* 5 (2009): 22–24.

[3] John Waters, "An Infinite Energy that Could Destroy Itself," *Traces* 1 (2011): 12.

[4] Pierre Teilhard de Chardin, *The Phenomenon of Man* (New York: HarperCollins Publishers, 2002), 232.

[5] Ernest L. Fortin, "The Regime of Separatism: Theoretical Considerations of the Separation of Church and State," in *Human Rights, Virtue, and the Common Good*, Ernest L. Fortin (Lanham, MD: Rowman and Littlefield Publishers, 1996), 8.

[6] Diane Ravitch, *The Death and Life of the Great American School System* (New York: Basic Books, 2010), 224.

[7] Hanna Arendt, *Between Past and Future* (1954; repr., New York: Penguin Books, 2006), 175.

[8] Reinhold Niebuhr, *Moral Man and Immoral Society: A Study in Ethics and Politics* (New York: Charles Scribner's Sons, 1934), xiii.

[9] Einstein, *Ideas and Opinions*, 52.

[10] Luigi Giussani, *La Conciencia Religiosa en el Hombre Moderno* [Religious Awareness in Modern Man] (Madrid, SP: Ediciones Encuentro, 1990), 46.

[11] Ibid., 19.

[12] Ibid., 44.

[13] Ravitch, *Death and Life*, 11.

[14] Walter Feinberg and Jonas F. Soltis, *School and Society* (New York: Teachers College, Columbia University), 23.

[15] Ibid., 26.

[16] Arendt, *Past and Future*, 183–184.

[17] Ibid., 191.

[18] Luigi Giussani, *The Risk of Education* (New York: The Crossroad Publishing Company, 2001), 7.

[19] Eddo Rigotti, *Conoscenza e Significato* [Knowledge and Meaning] (Milan, IT: Mondadori Università, 2009), 11.

[20] John Dewey, *Democracy and Education*, (1916; repr., Lexington, KY: Feather Trail Press, 2009), 67.

[21] Lawrence A. Cremin, *Traditions of American Education*, (New York: Basic Books, 1977), 94.

[22] Christopher Dawson, *The Crisis of Western Education* (1961; repr., Washington, DC: The Catholic University of America Press, 2010), 79.

[23] Maria Zambrano, quoted in Carlo M. Fedeli, *L'educazione come Esperienza* [Education as Experience] (Rome, IT: Aracne editrice, 2008), 7.

[24] Luigi Giussani, *La Conciencia Religiosa en el Hombre Moderno* [Religious Awareness in Modern Man] (Madrid, SP: Ediciones Encuentro, 1990), 40.

[25] Thomas Aquinas, *Summa Theologiae*, I, 76, 3.

[26] Augustine, *De Civitate Dei*, XIV, 3, 1.

[27] Jacques Maritain, *Education at the Crossroads* (1943; repr., New Haven, CT: Yale University Press, 1971), 9.

[28] Romano Guardini, quoted in Fedeli, *L'educazione*, 149.

[29] George Steiner, *Lessons of the Masters*, (Cambridge, MA: Harvard University Press, 2005), 18.

[30] Luigi Giussani, *The Risk of Education* (New York: The Crossroads Publishing Company, 2001), 105.

[31] Luigi Giussani, *The Religious Sense* (Montreal: McGill-Queen's University Press, 1997), 12.

[32] Giussani, *Risk*, 105.

[33] Rigotti, *Conoscenza*, 36.

[34] John H. Newman, *The Idea of a University Defined and Illustrated: In Nine-Discourses Delivered to the Catholics of Dublin* (1852; repr., Lexington, KY: Filiquarian Publishing LLC, 2011), 85.

[35] Maritain, *Crossroads*, 19.

[36] Ibid., 13.

[37] E. D. Hirsch, Jr., *The Making of Americans: Democracy and Our Schools* (New Haven, CT: Yale University Press, 2009), 45.

[38] Hanna Arendt, *Between Past and Future* (1954; repr., New York: Penguin Books, 2006), 180.

[39] John Locke, *Some Thoughts Concerning Education* (1693; repr., Indianapolis: Hackett Publishing Company, 1996), 40.

[40] Ibid., 51.

[41] Albert Einstein, *Ideas and Opinions* (New York: Three Rivers Press, 1954), 66.

[42] Diane Ravitch, *The Death and Life of the Great American School System* (New York: Basic Books, 2010), 224.

[43] Romano Guardini, quoted in Fedeli, *L'educazione*, 158.

[44] Hirsch, *The Making of Americans*, 50-51.

[45] Edgar Morin, *La Cabeza Bien Puesta* [The Head Screwed on Right] (Buenos Aires, AR: Nueva Vision, 2008), 17.

[46] Robert Hutchings quoted in Maritain, *Crossroads*, 54.

[47] Newman, *Idea*, 37.

[48] Alasdair McIntyre, *God, Philosophy, Universities* (Lanham, MD: Rowman & Littlefield Publishers, Inc., 2009), 174.

[49] Newman, *Idea*, 34.

[50] Ibid., 37.

[51] Giussani, *Hombre Moderno*, 17-26.

[52] Francis Bacon, "Advancement of Learning," in *The Works of Francis Bacon*, (Cambridge, MA: Houghton, Mifflin, and Company, 1900), 223.

[53] Etienne Gilson, *From Aristotle to Darwin and Back Again. A Journey in Final Causality, Species, and Evolution* (1971; repr., San Francisco: Ignatius Press, 2009), 21–37.

[54] Ibid., 33.

[55] Giussani, *Hombre Moderno*, 26-30.

[56] Arendt, *Past and Future*, 260.

[57] Ibid., 262-268.

[58] Ibid., 263.

[59] Morin, *Cabeza*, 98.

[60] Ibid., 35-58.

[61] William James, quoted in Neil Postman, *The End of Education* (New York, NY: Vintage Books, 1996), 113.

[62] Massimo Borghesi, *Il Soggetto Assente* [The Absent Subject] (Castel Bolognese, IT: Itaca libri, 2005), 47-64.

[63] Giussani, *Risk*, 7.

[64] Newman, *Idea*, 35.

[65] McIntyre, *Universities*, 173-180.

[66] Blaise Pascal, *Pensées* (New York: Penguin Books, 1995), 97.

[67] Einstein, *Ideas*, 61.

[68] Reinhold Niebuhr, *Moral Man and Immoral Society: A Study in Ethics and Politics* (New York: Charles Scribner's Sons, 1934), 245.

[69] Neil Postman, *The End of Education* (New York: Vintage Books, 1996), 4-18.

[70] Charles L. Glenn, *The Myth of the Common School* (Oakland, CA: Institute for Contemporary Studies, 2002), 4.

[71] Ibid., 20.

[72] Ibid., 22.

[73] Ibid., 36.

[74] Cremin, *Traditions*, 19.

[75] Glenn, *Myth*, 84-85.

[76] Diane Ravitch, *The Great School Wars: A History of the New York City Public Schools* (Baltimore, MD: The Johns Hopkins University Press, 2000), 244.

[77] Cremin, *Traditions*, 94.

[78] Glenn, *Myth*, 205.

[79] Joseph Chamberlain quoted in Dawson, *Crisis*, 78.

[80] Ibid., 84.

[81] Postman, *End*, 3-36.

[82] Maritain, *Crossroads*, 3-18.

[83] Giussani, *Hombre Moderno*, 43.

[84] Ibid., 15.

[85] Newman, *Idea*, 78.

[86] John Dewey, *Experience & Education* (1938; repr., New York: Touchtone, 1997), 28.

[87] Ibid., 89.

[88] Ibid., 6.

[89] Ibid., 49.

[90] Joseph D. Novak and D. Bob Gowin, *Learning How to Learn*, (Cambridge, UK: Cambridge University Press, 2002), xi.

[91] Dewey, *Experience*, 89.

[92] Carlo M. Fedeli, *L'educazione come Esperienza* [Education as Experience] (Rome, IT: Aracne editrice, 2008), 170.

[93] Carmine di Martino, "Knowledge is Always an Event", in *Knowledge is Always an Event*, ed. Alberto Savorana (Rimini, IT: Foundation Meeting for Frienship amongst Peoples, 2009), 13.

[94] Ibid., 6-35.

[95] Ibid., 6-35.

[96] Luca Tampellini, "La Scienza Sperimentale di Ruggero Bacone" [The Experimental Science of Roger Bacon] in *Sulle Spalle dei Giganti* [On the Giants' Shoulders] ed. EURESIS (Milan, IT: Edizioni SEED, 2005), 49–51

[97] Hanna Arendt, *The Human Condition* (1958; repr., Chicago: The University of Chicago Press, 1998), 285-289.

[98] Jean Guitton, *Arte Nuova di Pensare* [New Art of Thinking] (1946; repr., Cinisello Balsamo, IT: Edizioni Paoline, 1991), 71.

[99] Luigi Giussani, *The Religious Sense* (Montreal: McGill-Queen's University Press, 1997), 43.

[100] Ibid., 59-69.

[101] Ibid., 70-79.

[102] John Dewey, *The Quest for Certainty* (London: George Allen and Unwin, 1930), 295.

[103] Giussani, *Sense*, 132.

[104] Albert Einstein, *Ideas and Opinions* (New York: Three Rivers Press, 1954), 11.

[105] Giussani, *Sense*, 145

[106] Einstein, *Ideas*, 40.

[107] Giussani, *Sense*, 8.

[108] Di Martino, *Knowledge*, 6-35.

[109] Ibid., 17.

[110] Einstein, *Ideas*, 292.

[111] Werner Heisenberg, quoted in Marco Bersanelli and Mario Gargantini, *From Galileo to Gell-Mann*, (West Conshohocken, PA: Templeton Press, 2009), 6.

[112] Luigi Giussani, *The Risk of Education* (New York: The Crossroads Publishing Company, 2001), 98.

[113] Ibid., 98-99.

[114] Dewey, *Experience*, 44.

[115] John H. Newman, *The Idea of a University Defined and Illustrated: In Nine-Discourses Delivered to the Catholics of Dublin*, (1852; repr., Lexington, KY: Filiquarian Publishing LLC, 2011), 80–81.

[116] Dewey, *Experience*, 69.

[117] Giussani, *Sense*, 6.

[118] Ibid., 6-11.

[119] Giussani, *Risk*, 19.

[120] Ibid., 102.

[121] Dante, *Inferno*, XV, 82-85.

[122] Giussani, *Risk*, 105-106.

[123] Luigi Giussani, *The Risk of Education* (New York: The Crossroads Publishing Company, 2001), 50–51.

[124] Hanna Arendt, *Between Past and Future* (1954; repr., New York: Penguin Books, 2006), 192.

[125] Julian Carron, ed., *Giussani: Vivere Intensamente il Reale* [Giussani: Living Reality Intensely] (Brescia, IT: Editrice La Scuola, 2010), 13.

[126] Julian Carron, "Sfida dell'educazione, sfida della libertà" [Educational Challenge, a Challenge to Freedom], *I Quaderni di Liberta' di Educazione* 12 (2007): 4.

[127] Giussani, *Risk*, 11.

[128] Ibid., 84.

[129] Albert Einstein, *Ideas and Opinions* (New York: Three Rivers Press, 1954), 56.

[130] Giussani, *Risk*, 52-53.

[131] Ibid., 8.

[132] Reinhold Niebuhr, *The Nature and Destiny of Man,* vol. 2 of *Human Destiny* (New York: Nisbet, 1943), 6.

[133] Christopher Dawson, *The Crisis of Western Education* (1961; repr., Washington, DC: The Catholic University of America Press, 2010), 5.

[134] Lawrence A. Cremin, *Traditions of American Education* (New York: Basic Books, 1977), 12.

[135] E. D. Hirsch, Jr., *Cultural Literacy: What Every American Needs to Know* (New York: Vintage Books, 1988), 31.

[136] Giussani, *Risk*, 55.

[137] Ibid., 55-56.

[138] Ibid., 64.

[139] Ibid., 134.

[140] Dante, *Inferno*, XV, 82-85.

[141] Giussani, *Risk*, 65.

[142] Ibid., 66-67.

[143] Arendt, *Past*, 187.

[144] George Steiner, *Lessons of the Masters* (Cambridge, MA: Harvard University Press, 2005), 1.

[145] Giussani, *Risk*, 111.

[146] Steiner, *Lessons*, 1.

[147] Giussani, *Risk*, 112

[148] Ibid., 125.

[149] John Locke, *Some Thoughts Concerning Education* (1693; repr., Indianapolis: Hackett Publishing Company, 1996), 66–67.

[150] Giussani, *Risk*, 19.

[151] Ibid., 129.

[152] Ibid., 9-11.

[153] Ibid., 67.

[154] Giussani, *Sense*, 3-33.

[155] Ibid., 12-22.

[156] Joseph D. Novak and D. Bob Gowin, *Learning How to Learn* (Cambridge, UK: Cambridge University Press, 2002), 19.

[157] Giussani, *Sense*, 28.

[158] Giussani, *Risk*, 68-69.

[159] Ibid., 24.

[160] Miguel de Cervantes Saavedra, *Don Quixote*, Second Part, Chapter LVIII.

[161] Giussani, *Sense*, 128-129.

[162] Giussani, *Risk*, 33.

[163] Dewey, *Experience*, 71.

[164] Steiner, *Lessons*, 2.

[165] Ibid., 2.

[166] Giussani, *Risk*, 140.

[167] Ibid., 73-74.

[168] Ibid., 74-76.

[169] Ibid., 76-77.

[170] Robert Evans, "The Culture of Resistance," in *The Jossey-Bass Reader on School Reform*, ed. Jossey-Bass (San Francisco: Jossey-Bass, 2001), 520.

[171] Eddo Rigotti, *Conoscenza e Significato* [Knowledge and Meaning] (Milan, IT: Mondadori Università, 2009), 33.

[172] Thomas J. Sergiovanni, *The Principalship* (Boston: Pearson Education, 2009), 257.

[173] Rigotti, *Conoscenza*, 64-67.

[174] John Carew Eccles, *The Human Mystery* (London: Routledge & Kegan Paul, 1984), 10.

[175] Novak and Gowin, *Learning*, 77-91.

[176] Morin, *Cabeza*, 115.

[177] Rigotti, *Conoscenza*, 67-68.

[178] See http://www.meetingrimini.org.

[179] Steiner, *Lessons*, 18.

[180] Robert J. Marzano, *Classroom Management that Works* (Alexandria, VA: ASCD, 2003), 41.

[181] Gordon A. Donaldson, *Cultivating Leadership in Schools* (New York: Teachers College, Columbia University, 2006), 11.

[182] Ibid., 26.

[183] Rigotti, *Conoscenza*, 57-58.

[184] Ibid., 38.

[185] See Sergiovanni, *Principalship*, 272.

[186] Steiner, *Lessons*, 16-17.

[187] Sergiovanni, *Principalship*, 272.

[188] Newman, *Idea*, 267.

[189] Locke, *Education*, 72.

[190] Albert Camus, *The First Man* (New York: Alfred A. Knopf, 1995), 146.

[191] Dante, *Purgatory*, XVII, 127-129.

[192] Steiner, *Lessons*, 184.

[193] Rigotti, *Conoscenza*, 90-91.

[194] Aristotle, *Rhet.* I, 1, 1355a, 21-22.

[195] Thomas Aquinas, *Summa Contra Gentiles*, I, 1., 37-43.

[196] Giussani, *Risk*, 119-120.

[197] Camus, *First*, 143-144.

[198] Giussani, *Sense*, 100.

[199] Carlo Rubbia, quoted in Bersanelli and Gargantini, *From Galileo*, 8.

[200] Newman, *Idea*, 65.

[201] Giacomo Leopardi, quoted in Giussani, *Sense*, 49.

[202] Konrad Lorenz, *The Waning of Humanness* (Boston: Little, Brown and Co., 1987), 209.

[203] Rigotti, *Conoscenza*, 94-95.

[204] Locke, *Education*, 74.

[205] McIntyre, *Universities*, 94-95.

[206] Novak and Gowin, *Learning*, 40-54.

[207] Rigotti, *Conoscenza*, 122-133.

[208] Nathalie Muller-Mirza, "Les Indiens Ont-Ils une Âme?" [Do Indians Have a Soul?], in "Rapport à l'Altérité, Compétences Dialogiques et Apprentissage,"[Relation to Otherness, Dialogic Skills, and Learning] *Cahiers de Psychologie et Education de l'Université de Neuchâtel*, 43 (2008): 7–16.

[209] Hugo Mercier, "Reason Seen More as Weapon Than Path to Truth," *New York Times*, June 14, 2011, http://nyti.ms/j4Luz4.

[210] Max Planck, quoted in Bersanelli and Gargantini, *From Galileo*, 30.

[211] Thomas Aquinas, *Summa Teologiae*, II-II.q.166, a.1.

[212] Dante, *Convivio*, Book II, Chapter XV.

[213] Augustine, *Confessions*, Book XIII, 27-42.

[214] Segiovanni, *Principalship*, 257.

[215] Einstein, quoted in Bersanelli and Gargantini, *From Galileo*, 115.

[216] See J. A. Kulik, "Evaluating the Effects on Teaching with Computers," in *Microcomputers in Early Education*, eds. G. Campbell and G. Fein (Reston, VA: Reston, 1984); J. A. Kulik, R. Bangert, and G. Williams, "Effects of Computer-Based Teaching on Secondary Students," *Journal of Educational Psychology* 75, no. 1 (1983): 19–26.

[217] See R. Clark, "Reconsidering Research on Learning from Media," *Review of Educational Research* 53, no. 4 (1983): 445–459; R. Clark, "Evidence for Confounding in Computer-Based Instruction Studies," *Educational Communications and Technology Journal* 33, no. 4 (1985): 249–262.

[218] Postman, *End*, 189-193.

[219] Rosario Mazzeo, Alessandro Panzarasa, and Stefano Vignati, *Per lo Sviluppo dell'io* [For the Growth of the Self] (Milan, IT: Edizioni Odon, 2007), 130–132.

[220] Ibid., 132-133.

[221] Diane Ravitch, *The Death and Life of the Great American School System* (New York: Basic Books, 2010), 238.

[222] Plato, *Laws*, Book VII.

[223] Locke, *Education*, 52.

[224] Rigotti, *Conoscenza*, xiii.

[225] Manuel Oriol, "Introducción," [Introduction] in *Los Retos del Multiculturalismo* [The Multiculturalism Challenges], eds. Javier Prades and Manuel Oriol (Madrid, SP: Ediciones Encuentro, 2009), 17–24.

[226] See various references in Todd Whitaker and Douglas J. Fiore, *Dealing with Difficult Parents and with Parents in Difficult Situations* (Larchmont, NY: Eye on Education, 2001).

[227] Arendt, *Past and Future*, 182.

[228] Locke, *Education*, 62.

[229] S. B. Sheldon, "Improving Student Attendance with School, Family, and Community Partnerships," *Journal of Educational Research* 100, no. 5 (2007): 267–275.

[230] C. M. Hands, "Circles of Influence: The Role of School-Community Partnerships in the Character Formation and Citizenship of Secondary School Students," *Alberta Journal of Educational Research* 54, no. 1 (2008): 50–64.

[231] J. L. Epstein and M. G. Sanders, "Prospects for Change: Preparing Educators for School, Family, and Community Partnerships," *Peabody Journal of Education* 81, no. 2 (2006): 81–120.

[232] Rigotti, *Conoscenza*, 21.

[233] Ibid., 28-31.

[234] Dewey, *Experience*, 78.

[235] Ibid., 77.

[236] Hirsch, *The Making of Americans*, 36.

[237] Ravitch, *Death and Life*, 226.

[238] Postman, *End*, 115-116.

[239] Hans Freudenthal, *Revisiting Mathematics Education: China Lectures* (Dordrecht, The Netherlands: Kluwer Academic Publishers, 1991), 176-178.

[240] Ravitch, *Death and Life*, 237.

[241] Plato, quoted in Steiner, *Lessons* , 103.

[242] Freudenthal, *Mathematics*, 49-50.

[243] Ibid., 46-50.

[244] M Suzanne Donovan and John D. Bransford, eds., *How Students Learn Mathematics in the Classroom* (Washington, DC: The National Academies Press, 2005), 7.

[245] Alfred N. Whitehead, *Science and the Modern World* (1925; repr., New York: The Free Press, 1967), 31.

[246] Freudenthal, *Mathematics*, 41-42.

[247] Raffaella Manara, *La Matematica e la Realtà* [Mathematics and Reality] (Genoa, IT: Marietti, 2008), 135-154.

[248] Bersanelli and Gargantini, *From Galileo*, 17.

[249] Roger Bacon, quoted in Luca Tampellini, "La Scienza Sperimentale di Ruggero Bacone" [The Experimental Science of Roger Bacon] in *Sulle Spalle dei Giganti* [On the Giants' Shoulders], ed. EURESIS (Milan, IT: Edizioni SEED, 2005), 49.

[250] Ennio de Giorgi, quoted in Bersanelli and Gargantini, *From Galileo*, 196.

[251] Richard Courant, Herbert Robbins, and Ian Stewart, *What is Mathematics?* (Oxford, UK: Oxford University Press, 1996), 249.

[252] Einstein, *Ideas*, 231.

[253] Rabelais, quoted in Jacques Maritain, *Education at the Crossroads* (1943; repr., New Haven, CT: Yale University Press, 1971), 20.

[254] Erwin Schrödinger, "What Is Matter?" in *The Scientific American Book of the Cosmos*, ed. David H. Levy (New York: Byron Preiss, 2000), 27–28.

[255] Carl Sagan, *Cosmos* (New York: The Random House Publishing Group, 1985), 1.

[256] Thomas H. Huxley, quoted in Sagan, *Cosmos*, 1.

[257] Etienne Gilson, *From Aristotle to Darwin and Back Again. A Journey in Final Causality, Species, and Evolution* (1971; repr., San Francisco: Ignatius Press, 2009), 1–2.

[258] Eccles, *Mystery*, 10.

[259] Herodotus of Halicarnassus, *Persian Wars*, Book 1.

[260] Charles Péguy, *Basic Verities: Prose and Poetry* (New York: Pantheon Books, 1948), 83-85.

[261] Jose Rodelgo-Bueno, *Empresariado Social: del Estado Benefactor a la Sociedad del Bienestar* [Social Entrepreneurship: From the Welfare State to the Welfare Society] (San Juan, PR: Editorial Tal Cual, 2004), 95–101.

[262] Fyodor Dostoevski, *Demons* (New York: Penguin, 2008), 537.

www.ingramcontent.com/pod-product-compliance
Lightning Source LLC
Chambersburg PA
CBHW030006290326
41934CB00005B/246